Miracles in Mark

Miracles in Mark

DAVID SPELL

RESOURCE *Publications* • Eugene, Oregon

MIRACLES IN MARK

Copyright © 2009 David Spell. All rights reserved. Except for brief quotations in critical publications or reviews, no part of this book may be reproduced in any manner without prior written permission from the publisher. Write: Permissions, Wipf and Stock Publishers, 199 W. 8th Ave., Suite 3, Eugene, OR 97401.

Resource Publications
A Division of Wipf and Stock Publishers
199 W. 8th Ave., Suite 3
Eugene, OR 97401
www.wipfandstock.com

ISBN 13: 978-1-60608-406-9

Manufactured in the U.S.A.

*To Annie—
I look forward to the next
25 years.*

Contents

Introduction ix

1. A Sign from Heaven? 1
2. The Commissioning 4
3. The Capernaum Demoniac 10
4. Peter's Mother-in-Law 19
5. The Whole Town Gathered at the Door ... 21
6. A Man with Leprosy 23
7. The Healing of the Paralytic 29
8. A Healing in the Synagogue 34
9. Healings by the Lake 37
10. Sleeping through and then Calming the Storm 39
11. The Gerasene Demoniac 43
12. Touching Jesus in the Crowd 50
13. Waking up a Little Girl 54
14. The Feeding of the 5,000 59
15. Walking on the Water 64
16. Healings at Gennesaret 68
17. Feeding the Dogs under the Table 70
18. Healing a Deaf Mute 74
19. The Feeding of the 4,000 78
20. The Two Touch Healing 81
21. The Transfiguration 85
22. A Demon Possessed Boy 91

23 The Healing of Bartimaeus 97
24 Cursing a Fig Tree 101
25 God's Greatest Sign 107
26 The Resurrection 114

Bibliography 119

Introduction

WHY DO we need another study based on the Gospel of Mark? It has been one of the most exhaustively studied of the Gospels.[1] This study on the miracles and supernatural events in Mark is designed to provoke fresh discussion on Mark's reasons and intentions behind writing his book. The supernatural experiences in the book, as well as the miracles that Jesus performs, are very important to the structure of Mark. Why does Mark include the ones that he does? How does he use these stories in his narrative?

Miracles and supernatural experiences play a very important role in Mark's Gospel. He records seventeen individual miracles of Jesus and summarizes a number of others.[2] Mark devotes more space proportionally to miracles and supernatural experiences than any other Gospel. Taken as a whole, a third of Mark's Gospel is devoted to miracles. If we leave out the passion and just survey the first ten chapters, 200 out of 425 verses deal directly or indirectly with miracles.[3]

As with any study of Scripture, we do not just want to understand what the writer intended to say to his original audience. We also want to understand what spiritual truths lay hidden in the pages, waiting to be mined through prayer and study. This discussion will examine the miracles and supernatural experiences in both contexts. We will attempt to get the feel of what a first century believer might have felt when hearing these stories for the first time. We will also look for fresh ways in which we can apply the truths of Scripture in our modern context.

---

1. Hawkin, "Incomprehension," 491. "From the mid-nineteenth century until the publication of in 1901 of William Wrede's *Das Messiasgeheimnis in den Euangelien*, Mark was studied almost exclusively from the standpoint of historical Jesus research."

2. Brooks, *Mark*, 51–52.

3. Richardson, *The Miracle Stories*, 36.

Introduction

While the teaching of Jesus is important, it will not be the primary focus of this study. There will be references to certain teachings and parables, but our main focus will be on what Jesus did. We will look beyond the miracles, when applicable, to the message that we can apply to our lives. As Jeffrey John puts it so clearly, "All the miracle stories contain profound teaching which is of indispensable relevance to Christians and the Church today..."[4] We will look for that message as we study the miracles in Mark's Gospel.

David Spell

---

4. John, *The Meaning*, 25.

1

A Sign From Heaven?

The Pharisees came and began to question Jesus. To test him, they asked for a sign from heaven. He sighed deeply and said, "Why does this generation ask for a miraculous sign? I tell you the truth, no sign will be given to it."

(MARK 8:11–12)

MARK'S GOSPEL is full of miracles and supernatural experiences. Jesus performs many spectacular healings. He raises a dead girl from the dead. He demonstrates His power over nature by calming violent storms and walking on water. He miraculously feeds groups of five thousand and then four thousand people. Mark shows Jesus casting demons out of people in various settings. Most of the miracles that Mark presents are performed in a public setting. This particular interaction with the Pharisees occurred right after Jesus had fed the crowd of four thousand with seven loaves of bread and a few small fish.

The Pharisees and other religious leaders have had ample opportunities to see Jesus in action. In spite of this, they still want him to perform a "sign from heaven." The word that Mark uses here for "sign" is *sēmeion*, and is rarely used in this Gospel. By way of contrast, this is the favorite word used for miracles in John's Gospel.[1] What the Pharisees are seeking here is not another healing or exorcism or miraculous feeding. They are seeking an, "apocalyptic manifestation that would prove beyond all doubt that Jesus had God's approval."[2] The

---

1. John presents the miracles in a different way from the synoptic writers. He only presents seven miracles in his Gospel and they are presented as *sēmeions*, signs pointing to Jesus's divinity.

2. Brooks, *Mark*, 127.

MIRACLES IN MARK

type of sign that they are seeking is as much an evidence of trustworthiness as it was about power.[3] "They regard Jesus' miracles as ambiguous actions whose meaning must be confirmed by a sign."[4]

Perhaps the Pharisees are seeking a sign of the type that Moses performed before the Pharaoh. Perhaps they were thinking of Elijah and his showdown with the priests of Baal in which Elijah called down fire from heaven. The very fact that the Pharisees were seeking a sign from Jesus is interesting. Most of the religious leaders seem to have already made their minds up about Jesus. They accused Jesus of being in league with Satan in 2:22. There have been several other conflicts in which the Pharisees confronted Jesus over His supposed violations of the Law of Moses. In 3:6, the religious leaders, including the Pharisees are already plotting to kill Jesus. In all likelihood, the Pharisees are hoping that Jesus will attempt to perform some type of spectacular sign and fail. This would allow them to publicly discredit Him.[5]

This demand from the Pharisees for a sign actually highlights the many miracles and signs that Jesus has already performed. The very fact that the Pharisees have to ask for further signs is indicative of their own lack of faith and spiritual insight. In reality, one more sign is not going to change their minds.

Jesus makes it very clear that he does not perform miracles or signs on demand. By way of reply to the Pharisees, Jesus asks, "Why does this generation ask for a miraculous sign?" He seems to be saying, "Look at what I have already done. That should be enough." The miracles that He has already performed should be sufficient to convince someone who has an open heart and has not already rejected Jesus.

There also seem to be two other reasons why Jesus does not perform miracles on demand.[6] The first reason has to do with why Jesus *does* perform miracles. Mark shows Jesus performing miracles primarily in response to human need. "The miracles, like the teaching, of Jesus were not offered as signs convince spectators; they were

---

3. Lane, *Mark*, 277.
4. Ibid.
5. Hendriksen, *Mark*, 315.
6. English, *The Message of Mark*, 154.

done as acts of love to people in need."[7] In many ways, the words that Jesus spoke to Jairus after he was told his daughter was dead: "Don't be afraid; just believe," convey His attitude to humanity. Another window into Jesus's soul is found in Mark 8:2 where He speaks of the multitude but could be talking about all of lost humanity, "I have compassion for these people; they have already been with me three days and have nothing to eat." Mark clearly portrays Jesus performing miracles because of His compassion and love for humanity.

The second reason that Jesus did not perform miracles on demand was the fact that those who were asking came with the wrong attitude. They had come to "test him." This attitude would never lead to faith. The miracles that Jesus performed "became signs for those with the humility and openness to perceive and receive their meaning."[8] In a very real sense, Jesus's opponents are incapable of recognizing true signs and believing because they have already attributed His ministry to the Devil.[9]

After this encounter with the Pharisees, Jesus would continue to perform miracles. Mark records a number of other powerful healings and exorcisms. It will be in the next chapter where Mark will record the story of the Transfiguration. This was probably the very type of sign that the Pharisees were seeking. This experience, however, is reserved for only three select disciples. As we will see later, the greatest public sign of Jesus's ministry will be the cross. It like, all the others, can only be understood through the eyes of faith.

---

7. Ibid.
8. Ibid.
9. Schmidt, *The Gospel of Mark*, 92.

2

The Commissioning

At that time Jesus came from Nazareth in Galilee and was baptized by John in the Jordan. As Jesus was coming up out of the water, he saw heaven being torn open and the Spirit descending on him like a dove. And a voice came from heaven: "You are my Son, whom I love; with you I am well pleased.

(MARK 1: 9–11)

PUBLIC OR PRIVATE?

THIS FIRST miraculous or supernatural story in Mark is one of the two that seems to come the closest to the type of "sign" that the Pharisees demand in chapter eight. The other is the account of the Transfiguration. Both of these experiences involve visions, heavenly voices and supernatural phenomena designed to identify Jesus as the Messiah.

One of the first issues that must be considered is whether or not this experience was a public or private event. It could be argued that this sign was a public sign, whereas the Transfiguration was a private sign, seen only by Jesus and three of His closest disciples. This seems to be the way that the Baptism experience is presented in the other three Gospels. However, scholars such as James Brooks contend that Mark presents the Baptism experience as a private sign for Jesus only.[1] He feels that Mark's implication that Jesus alone experienced the supernatural phenomena (the heaven's opening, the Spirit descending, the heavenly Voice) gives the first hint of the secrecy motif. "The true identity of Jesus is concealed from the characters of the story, but not

---

1. Brooks, *Mark*, 43.

from the readers/hearers."[2] Kelber agrees when he writes, "Neither crowds nor John observe these extraordinary occurrences. Jesus' reception of the Spirit is an act of the greatest privacy, inaccessible to outside witnesses."[3] Mark implies that only Jesus saw the heavens opening and the Holy Spirit descending. The heavenly voice is in the first person, "You are my Son ..."

As mentioned above, the other Gospels seem to present the baptism experience and accompanying supernatural signs as a public event. Matthew's account of this event has God speaking in the third person, "This is my Son, whom I love; with him I am well pleased," (Matt.3: 17). Here, God seems to be addressing the onlookers. Luke's account of Jesus' baptism emphasizes the fact that Jesus was part of the crowd being baptized by John, "When all the people were being baptized, Jesus was baptized too," (Luke 3: 21). Luke emphasizes that Jesus's baptism was a public event. It did not take place in a private setting. In John's Gospel, John the Baptist testifies, "I saw the Spirit come down from heaven as a dove and remain on him," (John 1: 32). John himself saw the Holy Spirit come upon Jesus in the form of a dove. Taken together, the other Gospel accounts make a strong case that this was a public event.

Some scholars argue that the baptism was a public event. Donald English notes, "so surely the accompanying phenomena (the vision and the voice) are meant to be understood as public signs."[4] While this may be a valid argument if we are going to look at all the Gospels together, a study of Mark by itself leads to a different conclusion. Mark presents this story with Jesus alone being the recipient of the divine vision. This is Jesus's private commissioning from God. The reader/hearer is also allowed to partake later. For the people standing around, however, God's greatest sign will be reserved for the end of Jesus's ministry.

---

2. Ibid. See also Lane, *Mark*, 58, "Jesus' baptism must be seen from the aspect of his self-concealment. He was baptized as any other person who came to John. There is no indication in Mark that anyone other than Jesus understood the significance of the event."

3. Kelber, *Mark's Story*, 18–19. See also, Harrisville, *The Miracle of Mark*, 74.

4. English, *The Message of Mark*, 40. English continues, "On the threshold of his ministry the private disclosure to Jesus of his identity and the public testimony to him took place simultaneously."

MIRACLES IN MARK

SEARCHING FOR MEANING

The next question that we will explore is the meaning of the vision that Jesus had at his Baptism. The language that Mark uses is quite graphic. The first thing that Jesus saw was, "heaven being torn open." The word that Mark uses here is a form of *schisma*. This word is closely related to the one that he uses in describing the curtain in the temple being, "torn in two from top to bottom." (Mark 15: 38) Our English word *schism* is derived from this Greek word and helps to give us an idea of what Mark is saying.[5] This is not a picture of the curtains gently parting in the breeze, allowing Jesus to see into eternity. They were violently ripped apart. We will deal with curtain in the temple in more detail later, but Mark seems to use to use these two events as the frame that contains his story.[6] The heavens are ripped apart at the start of Jesus's ministry signifying a new period of revelation. The curtain is ripped apart at Jesus's death signifying that His work was finished and He has made a way for all people to have access to God, "by the blood of Jesus, by a new and living way opened for us through the curtain, that is his body," (Hebrews 10:19–20). This torn curtain will be discussed in more detail in a later chapter.

The open heavens are symbolic of divine revelation. Isaiah 64:1 invokes the Lord to, "rend the heavens and come down." Isaiah's vision of the Lord on His eternal throne provides us with a dramatic Old Testament prophetic calling. Rather than seeing Yaweh seated on His throne, however, Jesus sees the Holy Spirit, in the form of a dove, coming down from heaven upon Him. Ezekiel tells us that on the day he received his prophetic call, "the heavens were opened and I saw visions of God." (Ezekiel 1:1) There seems to be a strong connection between the vision that Jesus experiences at His baptism and that of the Old Testament prophets.[7] This was the specific time that Jesus received His call and commission from God. This was evidently the point where Jesus clearly understood God's divine purpose for His life.[8]

The next aspect of this vision that Mark describes is the descent of the Holy Spirit on Jesus in the form of a dove. This is a clear allu-

---

5. The root word is *Schisma*
6. Juel, *Mark*, 35.
7. Hurtado, *Mark*, 20.
8. Ibid., 19.

The Commissioning

sion to Isaiah 61:1, "The Spirit of the Sovereign Lord is upon me . . ." In Luke's Gospel this is the text for the first synagogue sermon that Jesus preaches after His baptism and wilderness temptation. Mark only alludes to the temptation period in the wilderness.[9] He does have Jesus preaching in a synagogue right after the baptism and temptation period but he does not give us the content of the message. What Mark does, however, is to demonstrate the fact that the Spirit of God is on Jesus as He performs an exorcism in the synagogue, setting a demon possessed man free. It is possible that Jesus preached on this passage from Isaiah 61 at the synagogue. What is important to Mark, however, is what Jesus did, not what He said. This exorcism story will be the subject of the next chapter.

The anointing of the Holy Spirit is almost always an aspect of divine commissioning. When Samuel anointed David with oil, "the Spirit of the Lord came upon David with power," (1 Samuel 16:13). Ezekiel said, "The Spirit came into me and raised me to my feet," (Ezekiel 2:2). The prophet Micah said, "But as for me, I am filled with power, with the Spirit of the Lord . . ." (Micah 3:8). The Scriptural pattern is that the Holy Spirit empowers, equips, and enables His servants to complete the mission that He has assigned them.

The picture of the dove is not as easy to understand. Did Jesus see a literal dove descending or was it a figurative description? Juel sees here a possible allusion to Genesis 1:2 where the Holy Spirit was "hovering" over the waters.[10] Here, the Holy Spirit is portrayed as hovering over and then coming to rest on Jesus. If this imagery is accurate, the picture is not one of a gentle christening! In Genesis, the Spirit was, "present with enormous creative force."[11] While every encounter with the Holy Spirit does not involve physical manifestations, there are many occasions that they do occur. The book of Acts is filled with powerful divine encounters. On the Day of Pentecost, the believers experienced the, "sound like the blowing of a violent wind . . . and then saw tongues of fire that separated and came to rest on each of them," (Acts 2:2-3).[12] On another occasion, after the believers prayed

---

9. Garrett, *Temptations*, 56-57. Garrett makes the case that Mark's entire Gospel deals with Jesus being tested.

10. Juel, *Mark*, 35.

11. English, *The Message of Mark*, 40.

12. Spell, *Peter and Paul*, 162-63. Luke seems to draw the comparison

MIRACLES IN MARK

together, "the place where they were meeting was shaken. And they were all filled with the Holy Spirit and spoke the word of God boldly," (Acts 4:31).

Hurtado, on the other hand, sees the image of a dove as comparative only.[13] Mark is using the dove imagery to describe the gentle way that the Holy Spirit comes upon Jesus. The dove occupies a key role in the flood story in Genesis. Noah releases a dove from the ark to see if it finds land. It returned to the ark "because it could find no place to sets its feet because there was water over all the surface of the earth," (Genesis 8:9). A week later, Noah sent the dove out again and it returned carrying an olive leaf in its beak. After seven more days, Noah released the dove again. This time it did not return, signifying that the waters had receded.[14]

Throughout the Scriptures, the dove is used to signify purity, gentleness, peacefulness, and graciousness. These characteristics are also representative of the Holy Spirit.[15] The Greeks regarded the dove as a divine bird, so Mark's readers would have quickly picked up on the references to divinity that he made here.[16] Whether intentional or not, Mark seems to acknowledge the doctrine of the trinity in this passage.[17] Jesus is baptized, the Holy Spirit comes to rest on Him, and the Father speaks.

The heavenly voice announces to Jesus, "You are my Son, whom I love; with you I am well pleased." There are three Old Testament passages that seem to be alluded to here. The first is from Psalm 2:7, "You are my Son, today I have become your Father." This Psalm was eventually used during the coronation ceremony for Jewish kings.[18] The Psalm also had apocalyptic overtones. "By the first century, Jews had come to regard this Psalm as prediction of the coming King from

---

between Jesus's baptism and the outpouring of the Holy Spirit on the Day of Pentecost. Jesus saw visible manifestations and heard an audible voice. In the same way, the believers at Pentecost saw tongues of fire and heard the sound of a violent wind.

13. Hurtado, *Mark*, 24.
14. See Genesis 8: 10–12.
15. Hendriksen, *Mark*, 43–44.
16. Gundry, *Survey*, 132.
17. Ibid.
18. Brooks, *Mark*, 43.

the line of David who would arise to save Israel."[19] God seems to be announcing that Jesus is the new king.

A second Old Testament passage that comes to mind here is Genesis 22:2 where God told Abraham to "Take your son, your only son, Isaac, whom you love, and go to the region of Moriah." This passage emphasizes Abraham's love for his son before telling him to take Isaac and sacrifice him to God. Here at Jesus's baptism we get the first hint of the fate that awaits Him. Jesus is being designated as the second Isaac who will be sacrificed by His Father.[20] The difference is that there will be no substitute for Jesus as there was for Isaac. There will be no last minute reprieve for the Son of God.[21]

The third passage that is being alluded to by the heavenly voice is from Isaiah 42:1, "Here is my servant whom I uphold, my chosen one in whom I delight; I will put my Spirit on him and he will bring justice to the nations." Isaiah makes reference to the "servant" of Yaweh in several other places in his prophecy (52:13– 53:12). The heavenly voice seems to identify Jesus as the servant that Isaiah prophesied about.[22]

This supernatural experience which Jesus had at the Jordan River can be seen as a divine commission that launched Jesus's public ministry.[23] Throughout the rest of this Gospel, Jesus operates in a way that shows Him fulfilling His heavenly commission. In the next chapter, we will discuss Jesus authority over the kingdom of the Devil as He confronts a demon possessed man.

19. Juel, *Mark*, 35.

20. Martin, *Mark—Evangelist and Theologian*, 128. See also, Dowd and Malbon, "The Significance," 273–274.

21. Ibid, Dowd and Malbon.

22. Juel, *Mark*, 35.

23. Tannehill, "The Gospel of Mark," 61. "The Gospel of Mark is the story of the commission which Jesus received from God and what Jesus has done (and will do) to fulfill his commission."

3

The Capernaum Demoniac

> *Just then a man in their synagogue who was possessed by an evil spirit cried out, "What do you want with us, Jesus of Nazareth? Have you come to destroy us? I know who you are—the Holy One of God." "Be quiet!" Jesus said sternly. "Come out of him!" The evil spirit came out of him with a shriek.*
>
> (MARK 1:23-26)

AFTER THE vision/commissioning that Jesus received at His baptism, He spent forty days in the wilderness being tempted by Satan. Mark gives us no details of this temptation as both Matthew and Luke do.[1] Mark then tells us that Jesus began preaching, "The time has come. The kingdom of God is near. Repent and believe the good news!" (Mark 1:15). This is followed by a short narrative describing the calling of the first disciples.

The next miracle story that Mark presents is the account of an exorcism during a synagogue meeting. Mark sets the story up by telling the reader that Jesus went into the synagogue in Capernaum on a Sabbath and began to teach. We are not told what Jesus teaches. We are, however, told what the response of the synagogue's audience was to Jesus's teaching. "The people were amazed at his teaching, because he taught them as one who had authority, not as the teachers of the law," (Mark 1: 22)

The word used here for "amazed" is *ékplēsso*. Translated literally it means, "to strike out of one's wits, to astound, amaze."[2] In other words, Jesus's hearers were out of their senses with wonder and amazement at

---

1. See Garrett, *Temptations*, ibid.
2. Moulton, *Greek Lexicon*, 127.

The Capernaum Demoniac

his teaching.³ We do not know what Jesus teaches, but it makes quite an impression on those who hear Him!

In Luke's Gospel, one of the first places that Jesus preached was in the synagogue in Nazareth.⁴ It was here that Jesus chose as His text Isaiah 61:1:

> *The Spirit of the Lord is on me,*
> *because He has anointed*
> *me to preach good news to the poor.*
> *He has sent me to proclaim freedom for the prisoners and*
> *recovery of sight to the blind,*
> *to release the oppressed,*
> *to proclaim the year of the Lord's favor.*

It is possible that this was the text that Jesus preached in Capernaum as well. While the crowd in Nazareth took offense at the "hometown boy" preaching a pointed message in the synagogue, the audience in Capernaum was much more receptive to Jesus's teaching. If this was the message that Jesus preached in Capernaum, by casting the evil spirits out, Jesus was demonstrating that truly, the Spirit of the Lord was on Him.

Of course, the actual text of what Jesus spoke on in this first synagogue sermon is mere speculation. Mark was more concerned about the reaction of the crowd to Jesus' message and then His confrontation with the demon possessed man. Mark portrays Jesus not only teaching with authority, but also using that authority to set an oppressed man free. Perhaps Jesus had been preaching in the synagogue that, "The Kingdom of God was near." This may have led to the conflict with the evil spirits.

Before we proceed too far into examining this story, the actual concept of demon possession needs to be discussed. Many scholars brush demon possession off as ignorance and superstition. Hurtado says, "The accounts [of exorcisms] resemble descriptions of certain kinds of behavior labeled in modern medical language as particularly severe mental disorders."⁵ Harrisville echoes this thought when he says, "Since Mark knows nothing more of the origins of diseases than

---

3. Hendriksen, *Mark*, 63.
4. See Luke 4:14–ff.
5. Hurtado, Mark, 33.

his contemporaries, he undoubtedly attributes to demon possession illnesses which modern man would prefer to call mental-physical or psychosomatic."[6] Fuller flatly states, "Of course, we no longer believe in demons."[7]

Hendricksen, on the other hand, accepts the accounts of demon possession at face value. He believes that Jesus regularly interacted with people who were under the influence of demonic spirits and set them free. Henricksen does not believe, however, that demon possession or activity has continued down through history. He believes that demon possession was a phenomenon limited to the time frame of Jesus's earthly ministry and during the period in which the church was born.[8]

On the opposite end of the spectrum are scholars such as James Brooks. He believes that we should not brush off Scriptural accounts of demon possession too quickly. "As difficult as the concept of the demonic is for most people today, it cannot be satisfactorily treated as a primitive explanation for various kinds of physical and psychological illness. A better explanation is that there is much less evidence of the demonic today because Jesus won a decisive, although not yet total, victory over it."[9] English feels that the writers of Scripture should not be considered ignorant too quickly. "The gospel writers made a clear distinction between illness and demon possession."[10] This is seen clearly in Mark 3:20–22. In this passage, Jesus's family tries to take charge of Him because they feel that "He is out of his mind." The religious leaders then accuse Jesus of being possessed by Beelzebub. Mark seems to differentiate here between demon possession and someone who was not in their right mind.

In same way, Bock acknowledges that, "Those who work in other cultures where the demonic is more openly accepted speak openly about its presence and see more cases of demon possession than we do."[11] Could it be that the reason many scholars dismiss any hint of

---

6. Harrisville, *The Miracle of Mark*, 26.
7. Fuller, *Interpreting*, 120.
8. Hendriksen, *Mark*, 65.
9. Brooks, *Mark*, 50.
10. English, *The Message of Mark*, 56.
11. Bock, *Luke*, 243.

demonic activity in the world today is because they have not left the safe confines of their classroom or office and traveled to places where they might have the opportunity to see the power of God delivering those who are oppressed by Satan? Very few people who have been involved in Third World ministry have to be convinced that demonic forces are still active in the world today. Most can recount personal examples of seeing people set free from the power of the enemy. Theologian Wayne Grudem comments,

> Much of our western secularized society is unwilling to admit the existence of demons—except perhaps in "primitive" societies—and relegates all talk of demonic activity to a category of superstition. But the unwillingness of modern society to recognize the presence of demonic activity today is, from a biblical perspective, simply due to people's blindness to the true nature of reality.[12]

I have been involved in both missionary and pastoral minstry for almost thirty years. As a young man, I spent a year living in Ghana, West Africa, as a missionary. On several occasions, I saw people who were demon possessed and had the privilege of seeing some of them set free. I have also been involved in missionary work in Honduras, Costa Rica, Mexico, Romania, Austria, India, and have been back to Ghana several times. On numerous occasions, I have been present during situations where we found ourselves dealing with active, manifesting demonic forces.

I do not want to weary the reader with pages of personal stories from the mission field. I will share one, however, that I believe will be beneficial and will illustrate the point that I am trying to make. In 2001, I was in Ongole, India. I was teaching at a week long pastor's conference during the day and speaking in house churches and open air meetings in the afternoon and evening.

After finishing a meeting at a house church, I was just about to get into the taxi with my translator. We were approached by a well dressed, middle aged woman. She told us that she had heard we were in the neighborhood and asked if we would come to her house and pray for her. She explained that she was a school teacher in the local middle school and had been there for years. Her desire was to move

12. Grudem, *Systematic Theology*, 420.

into an administrative position but to do that she would need an advanced degree. She had an application in at a local university but she told us that it was a very difficult process to get in. There were about one hundred applications for every one position. With that in mind, she had sought us out to come and pray for her for God's favor.

We walked over to her house. She lived in a nice home just down the street from where we were at. We stood in the woman's living room. My translator, the woman, two other Indian team members and I were present. After I was clear about what we were praying for, I began to pray out loud with my translator interpreting what I was praying. No one was touching the woman. I prayed a pretty generic prayer for God's favor and blessing on this woman and her application at the university. I did not know whether or not she was a Christian, so I also prayed that God would shine His light on her and reveal Himself to her. As this was being translated, the woman began to moan and sway. She had her eyes closed. At this point, I sensed the demonic was starting to manifest in the woman.

We then began to pray specifically against whatever spirits might be at work in this lady. Without being touched, the woman continued to moan and sway, and then fell to the floor. She began to writhe like a snake across the floor. We took authority over the demonic forces that were being manifested. While we were praying, the woman continued to writhe and moan. After about twenty minutes of intense prayer, the woman became quiet and stopped moving. We sensed that whatever demonic forces had been there were gone.

As if coming out of a trance, the lady got off the floor and sat on her couch. She apologized to us and said that that had never happened to her before. She appeared embarrassed and asked us what had had happened to her. We attempted in very simple terms to explain to her that it was not a coincidence that she had sought us out for prayer. God loved her so much that He wanted to set her free and reveal Himself to her. I then asked her about her household idols. In India, every Hindu household has a shrine of some sort set up. These idols are prayed to and worshipped. When I asked about her idols, she took us into an adjacent room and showed us her household idols, set up in a small shrine.

We went back into the living room. I led the woman through a prayer of repentance and of committing her life to Christ. Being a Hindu, she was not involved in any church. We recommended the house church that I had spoken at earlier. I also explained to her that she needed to get rid of her household idols or else she might find herself in a similar situation. She was resistant to getting rid of her idols and we didn't push the issue. Idolatry is deeply ingrained in the Hindu culture. What we did do was set up a follow up session for the woman with one of the local pastors for counseling and discipleship.

This testimony and many others that I have been a witness to, are similar to situations that are recorded in the Scriptures. There are many books written by missionaries and ministers that recount similar exorcism stories. Modern accounts of demonic possession may not be conclusive proof for those who choose not to believe. For anyone who has experienced the demonic firsthand, however, no academic argument is going to convince them otherwise.

Having made a case for the reality of the demonic in the world, however, I do not want to discount the fact that there have been abuses. In some circles, people with legitimate mental and physical illnesses have had them misdiagnosed as being demonic in nature. Thankfully modern medicine and science have brought relief and healing to many. For those who are oppressed by spiritual forces, however, only the power of God can bring lasting healing.

We will now turn our attention to the text of Mark and examine this exorcism story in chapter one. As was mentioned previously, the people were astounded and amazed at Jesus's teaching. Mark seems to indicate that Jesus had not gotten very far into His message. Jesus, ". . . began to teach. Just then a man in their synagogue who was possessed by an evil spirit cried out . . ." The first aspect of this story that bears examination is the identity of the demon possessed man. Mark says that he was "a man in their synagogue." This almost seems to imply that he is a member of the synagogue. It is surprising that the first demons that Jesus encounters are in a synagogue. We might expect Him to encounter demons in the market place, or when He was eating with the "tax collectors and sinners," but instead it takes place in a religious setting, an environment of worship. Juel sees the irony of the situation. "The unclean spirit is in a holy place on a holy day, where it ought not to be."[13] Perhaps this is a commentary on the spiritual condition of the town of Capernaum that a demon

---

13. Juel, *Mark*, 41.

possessed man could worship in the synagogue comfortably until confronted by Jesus.[14]

It is possible that the demon possessed man was not a member of the synagogue. He may have just wandered in response to the excitement that Jesus brought to every community that He went into. On the other hand, is it possible that this person was, in fact, a member of the synagogue? Could someone who was demon possessed live in their community and come to the synagogue on the Sabbath and appear "normal" until Jesus showed up? Based on what the text seems to imply and on my personal experience, I would have to say that it is possible for someone who is possessed or oppressed by evil spirits to live normal lives until something triggers them and causes those spirits to manifest. In the story I related above, we had no clue that the woman was demon possessed until the spirits started manifesting during prayer. Over and over again, mostly in third world countries, but even occasionally in the Untied States, I have been in situations where I have seen "normal" looking people start manifesting demonic activity during intense worship or prayer.

If this man was member of the synagogue, it actually makes this encounter even more impressive. The Jewish teachers of the law had either never gotten any kind of reaction from the demon possessed man, or else they had not been able to help him. In all likelihood, their teaching was probably not of a type to provoke a reaction from the evil spirits.[15]

As Jesus was teaching, the man that was possessed cried out, "What do you want with us, Jesus of Nazareth? Have you come to destroy us? I know who you are—the Holy One of God?" At this point, the man is completely under the control of the demons. The man is unable to seek Jesus's help. The demons, however, recognize Jesus as a threat. They perceive what few people have been able to so far. It will not be until Jesus's crucifixion that a human being will refer to Jesus as the "Son of God."[16] In identifying Jesus's true identity, the demons

---

14. Cole, *Mark*, 114.

15. In the chapter on the Gerasenes demoniac, we will discuss the possibility that there are different types of demonic spirits and how people respond differently to possession/oppression.

16. Brooks, *Mark*, 51.

The Capernaum Demoniac

show more insight than the people that Jesus interacts with, including His disciples.

The questions that the demons ask Jesus are insightful. The first question, "What do you want with us, Jesus of Nazareth," can also be translated, "Why do you bother us?"[17] There seems to be a premonition of what is about to happen to them. The demons refer to Jesus as "Jesus of Nazareth," but it does not appear to be derisive. In the next question, "Have you come to destroy us?," the demon seems to be acknowledging Jesus's heavenly origins. This could also be translated, "Have you come from heaven into the world to destroy us?"[18] Schmidt's translation is, "Have you come to get rid of us?"[19] This is exactly what Jesus has come for: to destroy the works of darkness and to get rid of them.

The last thing that the demon says is, "I know who you are—the Holy One of God." This will be seen throughout Mark. Whenever Jesus encounters evil spirits, they recognize His divinity. This is an amazing declaration by an unclean spirit and one that is repeated throughout the Gospel. This recognition makes a strong argument for reality of demons. What special ability would a person with some type of mental illness have to recognize Jesus's divinity if that is all demon possession is? Being mentally ill does not equate to having spiritual insight!

For His part, Jesus orders the evil spirits to, "Be quiet! Come out of him." Schmidt's translation is, "Shut up and get out of him!"[20] This was an intense encounter, as contacts with the forces of darkness tend to be. Much has been written about the secrecy motif that is present in Mark. Jesus commands the demons to be quiet in all of His encounters with them; in other places He orders people not to talk about what He did for them. Here, Jesus will not accept an evil spirit's proclamation of His Lordship.

Jesus does not negotiate with the demons. "Jesus strikes no truce and offers no terms; he expels the demons with great authority."[21] The result is that, "The evil spirit shook the man violently and came out of

---

17. Hendriksen, *Mark*, 65.
18. Ibid.
19. Schmidt, *Gospel of Mark*, 49.
20. Ibid.
21. Hurtado, *Mark*, 28.

him with a shriek." The crowd, who at first were astounded by Jesus's teaching, are now even more astounded by what they have witnessed. Not only does He teach with great authority, He also demonstrates that authority over evil spirits. This exorcism establishes Jesus as a powerful and popular teacher.

This first miracle in Mark sets the stage for the rest of his Gospel. Jesus's first message was that, "The Kingdom of God is near." In this exorcism, Jesus is establishing the fact that He has come to destroy the kingdom of Satan and to establish the Kingdom of God. "Whatever authority the demonic forces may have had is crumbling before the authority of the Son of God."[22] Jesus has begun to dismantle the structure of Satan's kingdom. The final destruction will take place at the cross.

---

22. France, *Divine Government*, 47.

4

Peter's Mother-in-Law

> *As soon as they left the synagogue, they went with James and John to the home of Simon and Andrew. Simon's mother-in-law was in bed with a fever, and they told Jesus about her. So he went to her, took her hand and helped her up. The fever left her and she began to wait on them.*
>
> (MARK 1:29–31)

OF ALL the miracles that Mark records, this one is by far the most innocuous. It is not nearly as dramatic as the previous exorcism. The ramifications are not nearly as great as the healing of the leper or the raising of the young girl from the dead. In spite of all that, this healing provides us with some key insights into the personality of Jesus.

This fact that this miracle is not as dramatic as others, does not in any way belittle the importance of this healing. While a fever in our day is often an inconvenience that is treated with bed rest and medicine, in ancient times, a fever could be fatal. This was a very serious condition and Jesus wasted no time in dealing with it.

This healing is also important in a historical sense. This little story gives us some rare insight into the home life of one of Jesus's disciples. It lets us know that Peter was married and probably had a family. In fact, Peter was the only one of the Twelve to have a family member healed by Jesus.[1] It is reasonable to assume that others among the Twelve were also married and had families. This fact adds weight to Peter's statement, "We have left everything to follow you!"[2]

The first thing that we should notice about this miracle is the fact that it is performed on a woman. As one of the first miracles that Mark

---

1. Achtemeier, *Mark*, 108.
2. Mark 10:28.

records, Jesus is seen reaching out to a member of an often overlooked group in society, namely women. While this might not seem like much of an issue in our modern society, in first century Palestine, women were little more than property. Jesus's willingness to heal a woman showed that He was not going to be bound by all the norms of His day. "By including accounts of the healing of women as well as men, Mark implied that Jesus was concerned about all people, including those who had a lowly place in society."[3] In some of the subsequent miracles that we will examine, we will see Jesus, time and again, reaching out to those on the margins of society and healing them.

Another aspect of this healing that needs to be commented on is the simplicity of it. In Mark's account, Jesus merely took the sick woman by the hand and helped her up. At this, "The fever left her . . ." This is in contrast to the exorcism that had just taken place. In that situation, Jesus spoke (possibly even yelled) at the demons and cast them out. There is no indication that He touched the demon possessed man. Here, Jesus does not say a word; He just helps the sick woman out of bed. There is no mention of the woman's faith or of anyone else's faith for that matter. The touch of Jesus was enough to bring total healing. No theological point is made. We just see Jesus exercising His authority and healing someone who is suffering.

The last aspect of this story that we will mention is the aftermath of the healing. After the fever left her, "she began to wait on them." After being healed, she immediately begins to serve Jesus and those with Him. Richardson sees this as a moral exhortation: "Christians who have been delivered from the power of sin and restored to health should at once begin to use their blessings in the service of the Lord."[4] Those who have been recipients of God's love and power have a responsibility to share that same love and power with those around them.

---

3. Brooks, *Mark*, 52.
4. Richardson, *The Miracle Stories*, 76.

5

The Whole Town Gathered at the Door . . .

> *That evening after sunset the people brought to Jesus all the sick and demon-possessed. The whole town gathered at the door, and Jesus healed many who had various diseases. He also drove out many demons, but he would not let the demons speak because they knew who he was.*
>
> (MARK 1:32–34)

THIS PASSAGE forms a Markan summary to show that Jesus's healing ministry was much more extensive than he has room to record. There are several of these summaries throughout the Gospel. The miracles that Mark does include in his Gospel are just a few of the many that Jesus performed. John referred to Jesus's "other" miracles in his Gospel: "Jesus did many other miraculous signs in the presence of his disciples which are not recorded in this book . . . Jesus did many other things as well. If every one of them were written down, I suppose that even the whole world would not have room for the books that would be written."[1]

This was a busy day for Jesus! It was the Sabbath and He had taught in the synagogue. While teaching there, He had been interrupted by a demon possessed man. Jesus cast the unclean spirits out of him. From there, Jesus had gone to the home of Simon Peter where He had healed Simon's mother-in-law who was sick in bed with a fever.

Now that the sun has gone down and the Sabbath is officially over, people start arriving at Simon's home bringing the sick and those oppressed by evil spirits. Since this is a summary passage, Mark does not provide details for any of the healings. We can surmise that they are similar to the others that he records in the Gospel.

---

1. John 20:30 and 21:25.

MIRACLES IN MARK

In dealing with those who are demon possessed, Jesus continues His pattern of not allowing them to speak, "because they knew who he was." The irony continues to be evident. The demons know who Jesus is but the people have not perceived His true identity yet.

The Greek here seems to indicate that this type of scenario happens regularly to Jesus.[2] Whereas the Gospel writers record numerous individual healings and miracle stories, the fact of the matter seems to be that Jesus was constantly healing people and casting out demons. Mark, as well as the other Gospel writers, highlighted the ones that they felt were the most significant and recorded them for the edification of their readers.

If this was the constant pattern of Jesus's life and ministry, it is no wonder that the next passage refers to Jesus going off, "to a solitary place, where he prayed."[3] Jesus needed to refresh His spirit and keep focused on God's plan for His life. This is a beautiful example for us to follow. No matter how busy or successful that we become, we must constantly make time to spend in God's presence. Prayer and Scripture reading should be done to cultivate our relationship with Christ and to feed our spirit, not just to prepare our next sermon or lesson plan. In spite of the demands placed on His time, Jesus always made time for prayer.

2. Schmidt, *The Gospel of Mark*, 49.
3. Mark 1:35

6

A Man with Leprosy

> *A man with leprosy came to him and begged him on his knees, "If you are willing, you can make me clean." Filled with compassion, Jesus reached out his hand and touched the man. "I am willing," he said, "Be clean!" Immediately, the leprosy left him and he was cured. Jesus sent him away at once with a strong warning: "See that you don't tell this to anyone. But go, show yourself to the priest and offer the sacrifice that Moses commanded for your cleansing, as a testimony to them." Instead, he went out and began to talk freely, spreading the news.*
>
> (MARK 1:40–45)

THIS ACCOUNT of Jesus healing the leprous man is the first of several stories that show Jesus violating ritual boundaries.[1] People who had leprosy were considered to be ritually "unclean," as well as being sick. The man does not ask Jesus to heal him. He asks Jesus to make him clean. There was no known cure for leprosy.

The Torah sets down very strict guidelines concerning those who were afflicted with leprosy. "As long as he has the infection he remains unclean. He must live alone; he must live outside the camp."[2] While this seems harsh to our modern sensibilities, these guidelines were for the protection of society as a whole. Leprosy was not only viewed as being extremely contagious; coming into contact with a leper rendered one ritually unclean. Anyone touched by a leper would

---

1. Juel, *Mark*, 43.
2. Leviticus 13:46.

have to be quarantined until examined by a priest.[3] "Laws of ritual uncleanness thus served to protect the community from danger."[4]

The person that was afflicted with this type of disease was forbidden to enter the temple or participate in any type of social gathering. They were separated from the life of the community. They could only see their families from a distance and their only friends were those who suffered from the same malady. The life of a leper was a living death.

Those who were afflicted with leprosy were viewed as people that God had judged. A common biblical assumption was that the disease was "evidence of sinfulness."[5] They had done something that had brought this horrible disease upon them. They were suffering as a result of their sin. This was a commonly held belief in the first century. As the disciples asked Jesus in John, "Rabbi, who sinned, this man or his parents, that he was born blind?"[6]

The first aspect of this healing that catches our attention is the act of the leper approaching Jesus. Lepers were forbidden from having contact with people except from a distance. They were required to shout, "Unclean! Unclean!" whenever they approached anyone.[7] This would allow the unaffected person to get out of the leper's way.

Mark makes it clear here, however, that the leper deliberately approaches Jesus. Evidently, he had heard about Jesus's mighty works. He might even have seen him from a distance. He had enough knowledge of Jesus to know that Jesus had the power to make him clean. The leper seeks Jesus out and then confronts him. "It was shocking behaviour, which expresses the man's desperation about his plight and the strength of his faith."[8] This man had heard enough about Jesus that his faith had risen to a level that he was willing to break the cultural norm and directly approach Jesus.

The desperation of leprous man is obvious. What does he have to lose by approaching Jesus? He is already an outcast. What are they

3. John, *The Meaning*, 27.
4. Juel, *Mark*, 44.
5. Richardson, *The Miracle Stories*, 60.
6. John 9:2.
7. Leviticus 13:45.
8. John, Ibid.

going to do to him? Make him go and live in a leper colony? He really has nothing to lose by trying to get to Jesus and everything to gain.

As the man with leprosy approaches Jesus, he drops to his knees, and then says, "If you are willing, you can make me clean." The word that Mark uses here for kneeling, *gonupeteō*, not only carries the idea humility but also implies worship. The man obviously has faith or else he would not have approached Jesus in the first place. His faith, however, is wrapped in humility. The leper's statement to Jesus is confident but not demanding. He has taken the first step in making contact with Jesus. Now it is up to Jesus. How will He respond?

The NIV tells us that Jesus was "Filled with compassion," While most early manuscripts can be translated this way, there are several that have an alternate reading. Brooks notes that one Greek manuscript, four old Latin manuscripts and one early Christian author read that instead of being filled with compassion, Jesus "became angry."[9] This presents a problem for the scholar. Which manuscript is the correct one? What is the correct translation here? Jesus being filled with compassion seems to fit in better with our understanding of the nature and character of Jesus. Schmidt, however, translates this passage saying that "Jesus was indignant."[10] This reading is closer to Jesus being angry than being filled with compassion.

If the correct reading was "Jesus became angry," or "Jesus was filled with anger," who or what was He angry at? It is unlikely that He was angry at the leper. Jesus says later in Mark's Gospel, "For even the Son of Man did not come to be served, but to serve, and to give his life as a ransom for many."[11] The leper was exactly the kind of person who Jesus had come to serve. It seems likely that Jesus anger was directed, first of all, at a religious establishment that could do nothing to help this afflicted man. They could declare him unclean and they could declare him clean but they could not heal him. They showed little compassion for the outcasts of society.

---

9. Brooks, *Mark*, 55. "Despite the massive external attestation for "filled with compassion," internal considerations are so strong that "having become angry" probably is the original." See also English, *The Message of Mark*, 63.

10. Schmidt, *The Gospel of Mark*, 51.

11. Mark 10:45.

A second object of Jesus's anger would be, "at the evil which spoils human nature in any shape or form."[12] Jesus was angry at the evil force that had held this man prisoner for so long. This man's life has been destroyed by forces beyond his control. Jesus was moved to anger at how sickness had ravaged this leper's life.

Mark then tells us that Jesus touched the man and said, "I am willing. Be clean!" Even if the "with compassion" is not the correct translation here, Jesus demonstrates compassion by how He responds to the leprous man.[13] It was unheard of for a Jew to touch a leper. This act immediately rendered Jesus ceremonially unclean. Jesus' compassion is shown through His actions.

Why did Jesus have to physically touch this man? In many other locations, Jesus heals with only a word. It is reasonable to assume that He could have healed this man with a word, and thus, not have defiled Himself. Instead, Jesus purposely stepped over the ritual boundary to touch this man. The touch here from Jesus provides us with a window into the heart of God. Even though Jesus could have healed the man with a word, Jesus went a step farther and established social contact with the man. Jesus was welcoming him back into society. One can only speculate how long it had been since this man had had normal human contact. Jesus not only healed the man, He also let the man feel a human touch again. Instead of recoiling in horror, Jesus let the man know that he was loved and accepted.

The fear of touching a leper was not only that one would become ceremonially unclean, but it was that the leprosy was contagious and would spread to the one doing the touching. Here however, instead of the "contamination flowing from the leper to Jesus, healing power flows from Jesus to the leper."[14] Origen takes it a step further. He believes that the leper was healed at the word of Jesus. Then, "the hand of the Lord is found not to have touched a leper, but a body made clean!"[15]

In an instant, the man is cleansed. He is healed of his leprosy. The Torah specifies that he must now show himself to a priest to verify that he is really clean. Even though Jesus has demonstrated that He

12. English, *The Message of Mark*, 63.
13. Brooks, *Mark*, 55–56.
14. John, *The Meaning*, 28.
15. Oden and Hall, *Ancient Christian Commentary*, 26.

A Man with Leprosy

will break traditions and "violate sacred boundaries,"[16] He understands the importance of having the man's healing verified by a priest. This confirmation of his healing would allow the man to integrate back into society without delay. This would also provide a powerful testimony of Jesus's healing power to the religious establishment that He had so much conflict with.

The NIV says that, "Jesus sent him away at once with a strong warning." This passage also provides a bit of controversy in the way that it is translated. The Greek for "strong warning" is a term that is often used to describe the snorting of a war horse in battle.[17] The Greek word, *embrimaomai*, also carries the meaning of being, "greatly fretted or agitated . . . or to express indignation."[18] Again, this does not seem to fit with our understanding of the character and nature of Jesus. Hendricksen provides an alternate but possible reading of Jesus "was deeply moved in spirit."[19] Schmidt's translation seems to capture the essence of the Greek, "Jesus snapped at him and dismissed him curtly with this warning . . ."[20]

Again, the question can be asked, why is Jesus angry, impatient, agitated, etc.? The language that Jesus uses here is similar to that in other places where He performs an exorcism.[21] This does not really answer the question, however, of why Jesus appears to be angry or agitated with the man that He just healed.

Another possibility is that Jesus knew that the man would go and broadcast this miracle and that His "cover would be blown." Whether or not this was why Jesus was agitated, it was the ultimate result of the healing: "As a result, Jesus could no longer enter a town openly but stayed outside in lonely places."[22] Hurtado sees Jesus's anger directed

---

16. Juel, *Mark*, 44.
17. Achtemeier, *Invitation to Mark*, 44.
18. Moulton, *Greek Lexicon*, 134.
19. Hendriksen, *Mark*, 80.
20. Schmidt, *The Gospel of Mark*, 51.
21. John, *The Meaning*, 28–29. "From a Gospel point of view all sickness and disorder, as well as natural forces such as a storm, was as much evidence of demonic power as explicit possession. The language is therefore similar to that of an exorcism: Jesus is driving out a 'spirit of leprosy.'"
22. Mark 1:45.

at the healed man's disobedience.[23] Instead of going and showing himself to the priest as Jesus commanded "he began to talk freely, spreading the news." This is probably the best reason that has been put forth for Jesus' agitation.

In reality, however, this is a difficult passage. Juel's honesty is refreshing: "Mark does not provide enough information to understand why Jesus might be angry."[24] Achtemeier goes a step further when he says of this passage, "Jesus is a man possessed by God, and is strange even in his own world. To reduce him to a sentimental "friend in the garden" is blasphemous. To confront him is to confront the living God."[25]

C. S. Lewis shares a similar thought in *The Lion, the Witch, and the Wardrobe*. Lucy, after hearing about the Great Lion Aslan, asks the question, "Is he safe?" The answer comes from Mr. Beaver, "'Course he isn't safe. But he's good. He's the king I tell you."[26]

---

23. Hurtado, *Mark*, 31. "Though the man has been cured by Jesus and owes him obedience, he shows himself disobedient and devoid of genuine insight into Jesus' significance."

24. Juel, *Mark*, 44.

25. Achtemeier, *Invitation to Mark*, 45.

26 Lewis, *The Lion*, 80.

7

The Healing of the Paralytic

> *Some men came, bringing to him a paralytic, carried by four of them. Since they could not get him to Jesus because of the crowd, they made an opening in the roof above Jesus and after digging through it, lowered the mat the paralyzed man was lying on. When Jesus saw their faith, he said to the paralytic, "Son, your sins are forgiven." ". . . But that you may know that the Son of Man has authority on earth to forgive sins . . ." He said to the paralytic, "I tell you, get up, take your mat and go home." He got up, took his mat and walked out in full view of them all. This amazed everyone and they praised God, saying, "We have never seen anything like this!"*
>
> (MARK 2:3–5, 10–12)

THIS MIRACLE occurs in Capernaum. Mark tells us that it takes place, "A few days later." Jesus has returned from his travels in Galilee and has come back to the city that will become His base of operations. As in the first chapter of Mark where, "The whole town gathered at his door,"[1] so here, "So many gathered that there was no room left, not even outside the door."[2] There is no indication in the Gospels that Jesus had His own house, so the most likely location is again at Simon Peter's home.[3]

Like the exorcism in the synagogue, this miracle starts with Jesus teaching the crowd. Again, we are not privy to what Jesus was teaching the people. Mark just says that, "he preached the word to them." Mark gives us several examples of Jesus's teaching in other locations in His

---

1. Mark 1:33.
2. Mark 2:2.
3. Brooks, *Mark*, 58.

Gospel. What happens while Jesus is teaching is the real subject that Mark wants to discuss.

As Jesus is teaching, four men come carrying a fifth man who is paralyzed. They are unable to get to Jesus because of the crowd. They are determined, however, to get their friend in to Jesus. They manage to get on the roof of the house. Many houses in Palestine had steps that led to the roof. The four men then dig a hole through the roof to create an opening. Roofs in Palestine were made of tree branches and baked clay mixed with straw so this was not a difficult job.[4] It probably created quite a disturbance, however, while Jesus was teaching down below where they were digging!

The paralyzed man was then lowered on his mat down to Jesus. Mark notes that Jesus saw their faith. Their actions demonstrated their faith. The four friends, having completed their task, now disappear from the story. This is an interesting point. The friends have done the hard work. They carried their friend to the house where Jesus was and then up onto the roof. They dug the hole in the roof and then lowered the paralytic down to Jesus. It is their faith that Jesus notices.[5] Now that their job is finished, the reader's attention is focused on Jesus, the paralytic, and the religious leaders.

Jesus's response is to say to the man on the mat, "Son, your sins are forgiven." This is not what we would have expected Him to say. The reader would expect Jesus to say, "Rise and walk." Instead, Jesus tells him that his sins are forgiven. This pronouncement by Jesus brings up the issue of the relationship between sin and sickness. In this case, at least, Jesus seems to make some type of connection between the two.

Is sickness caused by sin? In John's Gospel, this very question comes up concerning the man born blind. "His disciples asked him, "Rabbi, who sinned, this man or his parents, that he was born blind?"[6] For the disciples, this is not even open for discussion. They believed that someone's sin caused the man to born blind. Jesus's answer, however, makes it clear that sin was not the cause of the man's blindness:

---

4. Hendriksen, *Mark*, 87–88.
5. John, *The Meaning*, 40.
6. John 9:2.

The Healing of the Paralytic

"Neither this man nor his parents sinned," said Jesus, "but this happened so that the work of God might be displayed in his life."[7]

The passage under consideration in Mark, however, points in a different direction. By telling him that his sins are forgiven before He heals him, Jesus implies a relationship between the sickness and the sin. Hendricksen, however, argues that this is an unwarranted implication.[8] In reality, though, this is the only healing that Jesus performs in which He starts off by addressing the person's sins before He heals them. As Juel states, "Jesus' words presuppose a link between sin and disease."[9]

Probably the safest assumption that we can make is that some sickness is caused by sin. There seems to be a Scriptural basis for this, as we have seen. At any rate, Jesus seemed to see a connection between this man's paralysis and his sin. Mark does not tell us what the sick man's reaction is to this pronouncement of his forgiveness. Instead, Mark lets the reader know what the religious leaders in the audience are thinking: "Now some teachers of the law were sitting there, thinking to themselves, 'Why does this fellow talk like that? He's blaspheming! Who can forgive sins but God alone?'"[10]

Mark then records that Jesus immediately knew what the religious leaders were thinking. Mark seems to indicate that Jesus received this knowledge supernaturally. There are many other examples throughout the Gospels where Jesus appears to read people's minds and know their thoughts.[11] As a Man, Jesus was certainly limited in many ways. He could not be everywhere at once, for example. His human body brought with it certain limitations. Jesus got tired and had to sleep. He had to eat and drink, etc. With these limitations, the issue of Jesus's knowledge and insight come up for discussion. Jesus, Himself, notes some limitation on His knowledge when He says, "No one knows about that day or hour, not even the angels in heaven, nor the Son, but only the Father."[12]

---

7. John 9:3.
8. Hendriksen, *Mark*, 88.
9. Juel, *Mark*, 46.
10. Mark 2:6–7.
11. Luke 7:39–ff; Luke 9:46–47; John 2:24–25.
12. Mark 13:32.

How then, did Jesus get His insight into what the religious leaders were thinking? The most likely answer is that He relied on the Holy Spirit to help Him and used the spiritual gifts that Paul described in his letters. In this case, the word of knowledge is probably how Jesus was able to know what the teachers of the law were thinking. Paul refers to the "word of knowledge" in 1 Corinthians 12:8. Morris points out that, "Paul associates *knowledge* with mysteries, revelations, and prophecy."[13] Paul understands this gift to be one in which the believer receives "supernatural mystical knowledge."[14] We saw in the first chapter of Mark that the Holy Spirit came and rested on Jesus. The Holy Spirit would have provided Jesus with supernatural insight into what people were thinking.

Now that Jesus knew what the teachers of the law were thinking, He called them on it. "Why are you thinking these things?"[15] He does not dispute their claim. They are right: only God can forgive sin. At the same time, Jesus does not feel the need to explain Himself or to defend His right to pronounce forgiveness.[16] He then asked an interesting question. "Which is easier: to say to the paralytic, 'Your sins are forgiven,' or to say, 'Get up, take your mat and walk'?"[17] Obviously, it is much easier to pronounce someone's forgiveness as opposed to telling a paralytic to get up and walk! Words are always easier than actions.

Jesus then said, "But that you may know that the Son of Man has authority on earth to forgive sins . . ." He then addressed the paralytic and told him, "I tell you, get up, take your mat and go home." The result was that the paralytic did exactly that "and walked out in full view of them all." The crowd was understandably amazed and "praised God saying, "We have never seen anything like this."

This miracle brings together forgiveness and physical healing. Fuller notes that they "are not two separate things, the one inward and spiritual, the other outward and physical. The remission of sins is the

---

13. Morris, *1 Corinthians*, 171.
14. Ibid.
15. Mark 2:8.
16. Juel, *Mark*, 48.
17. Mark 2:9.

The Healing of the Paralytic

total gift of salvation of which physical healing is a part."[18] Jesus came not just heal someone's body; He came to heal the whole person.

It is important to note here that this healing is not just a display of Jesus's authority to prove a point to the teachers of the law. Rather, this was exactly what Jesus came to do: forgive people and heal them. This is actually a beautiful picture of salvation. The paralyzed man is held in bondage by his sickness and confined to his bed just as we are in bondage to our sins. His healing "is a vivid picture of release from sins and guilt."[19] Salvation is healing. Jesus often uses the word for healing and salvation interchangeably.[20]

At the same time, however, it is clear that Jesus is claiming divine authority here to forgive sins.[21] He not only claims divine authority, He goes out of His way to prove it by performing the healing. The religious leaders clearly understood what Jesus was claiming. They do not see through the eyes of faith and see only a blasphemer. Many in the crowd, however, were moved to praise God.

In concluding our discussion on the healing of the paralytic, we will touch on a point that is often overlooked. Scholars have discussed the "Messianic secret" or the "secrecy motif" that some have seen in Mark's Gospel since early in the last century. In several places in the Gospels, Jesus commands people and demons to silence. It is evident that He does not want demons declaring His divinity. Jesus also commanded people that He healed not to tell what had happened. The leper that Jesus cleansed was one example. Another was the parents of the girl that Jesus raised from the dead in Mark 5:43. It is clear that at different times during His ministry, Jesus did tell people not to discuss what had happened to them. In this healing story, however, Jesus has no reservations about creating an incident in which He does something that only God can do (forgive sins) and then pointedly heals a man to demonstrate that His claim to be able to forgive sins is valid. He performs this miracle, not in secret, but in a crowded room. In this case, there was no command to secrecy.

---

18. Fuller, *Interpreting*, 51.
19. Hurtado, *Mark*, 37.
20. Mark 5:34; 10–52.
21. France, *Divine Government*, 101–102.

8

A Healing in the Synagogue

Another time he went into the synagogue, and a man with a shriveled hand was there. Some of them were looking for a reason to accuse Jesus, so they watched him closely to see if he would heal him on the Sabbath. Jesus said to the man with the shriveled hand, "Stand up in front of everyone." Then Jesus asked them, "Which is lawful to do on the Sabbath: to do good or to do evil, to save life or to kill?" But they remained silent. He looked around at them in anger and, deeply distressed at their stubborn hearts, said to the man, "Stretch out your hand." He stretched it out, and his hand was completely restored.

(MARK 3:1–5)

THIS HEALING miracle is described by some scholars as more of a "conflict and/or pronouncement story," rather than a story that emphasizes the healing itself.[1] Jeffrey John does not even mention this healing in his *The Meaning in the Miracles* book. The fact that this encounter takes place on the Sabbath right after another Sabbath encounter between Jesus and the Pharisees, has led many to conclude this is just another story detailing the conflict between Jesus and the religious leaders in regards to Sabbath observance.[2]

There is no question that this issue of Sabbath observance comes into play here. At the same time, it is important that we not minimize the importance of the miracle that is central to the conflict. There are several other healings that Mark records that take place on the Sabbath. As we see in all of them, Jesus does not shy away from conflict. He is intent on doing the right thing for the particular individual,

1. Brooks, *Mark*, 67. See also Fuller, *Interpreting*, 52–53.
2. See Mark 2:23–28.

A Healing in the Synagogue

no matter what restrictions the religious leaders have established in regards to the Sabbath. The common rabbinic position was that it was only permissible to heal someone on the Sabbath if their life was in danger.[3] By that standard, a shriveled hand would not be classified as life threatening. Jesus, however, refused to accept that standard.

The illness that Mark describes here is not completely clear in our English translations. The NIV says that the man's hand was "withered." The words "crippled" and "paralyzed" also convey the idea of the type of illness that Mark refers to. There has been some speculation that the man's hand is crippled because of some type of injury that he had received.[4] It is likely that the disability now kept him from working, especially if he was injured while working with his hands. Another important fact is that this type of injury would have kept the man from fully participating in the religious life of the community.[5] His defect meant that he was forbidden from entering the temple.[6] When Jesus healed him, the man was restored not only to health but also to social and religious acceptance.

As we have noted, this miracle takes place in the synagogue on the Sabbath. When Jesus saw the man with the crippled hand, He made a point of calling him out into the middle of the synagogue. Jesus could have avoided this situation by simply waiting until after the Sabbath to heal the man. As we noted above, however, Jesus did not accept the rabbinic rules regarding the Sabbath.

Jesus seems to use the man as a type of object lesson. When He brings him out into the middle of the synagogue, He asks the religious leaders, "Which is lawful to do on the Sabbath: to do good or to do evil, to save life or to kill?" Even though the rabbinic rule is that only life threatening injuries are eligible for a Sabbath healing, Jesus looks beyond the rule. As He so often does when interpreting the Law, He looks beyond the surface of the words to the spirit of the Law. Jesus's question "lifted the issue of Sabbath observance above a list of prohibitions to the higher general principle."[7] While the religious leaders

3. Hendriksen, *Mark*, 114.
4. Ibid.
5. Hurtado, *Mark*, 50.
6. Leviticus 21:16-24.
7. Brooks, *Mark*, 68.

only saw the Sabbath as day to refrain *from* things, Jesus understood the day to be an opportunity to actively *do* good things.

The question that Jesus asks is obvious in its answer. Jesus's opponents, however, refused to answer Him. They were experts in the nuances of the Law but Mark says "they remained silent." Mark again comments on Jesus being angry, but also mentions the fact that at the same time Jesus is distressed or grieved because of the hardness or stubbornness of their hearts. The word that Mark uses for anger is *orgēs*, referring "to the divine wrath expressed in opposition to evil."[8] Mark often portrays Jesus with these conflicting emotions, anger at the religious leader's judgmental attitudes and sorrow over their hard hearts.[9]

After getting no response from the religious authorities, He turns His attention back to the man with the crippled hand. He told the man, "Stretch out your hand." The man did so and "it was completely restored." In the sight of everyone in the synagogue, the man was instantly healed.

Nothing more is said about the healed man in this story. Mark's attention now focuses on the result of the healing: "Then the Pharisees went out and began to plot with the Herodians how they might kill Jesus." Jesus had asked them what it was lawful to do on the Sabbath. Was it lawful to do good or evil? Was it lawful to save a life or to kill? While Jesus was busy doing good on the Sabbath, the Pharisees and Herodians were using the Sabbath to plot Jesus's death.

The contrast here between the anger of Jesus and the anger of the religious leaders is interesting. Jesus's anger is unselfish and is tempered by His sorrow over their stubbornness. The anger of the Pharisees and other leaders, however, is focused on murdering Jesus as soon as the opportunity presents itself. They feel humiliated after seeing Jesus challenge and defeat their religious rules.[10] The fact that they have just observed Jesus perform a healing miracle makes no difference to them. Their hearts are hard and their eyes are blinded from perceiving Who Jesus is.

---

8. Martin, *Mark—Evangelist and Theologian*, 121.

9. Ibid.

10. Hendriksen, *Mark*, 117. See also, Juel, *Mark,* 56. "There was a good possibility that he [Jesus] would pull the whole structure down, making civilized life impossible, removing the last barrier to the wave of Hellenism that threatened to sweep Jewish tradition into oblivion. Jesus' Sabbath transgressions, however trivial they may appear to us, were genuinely dangerous."

9

Healings by the Lake

Jesus withdrew with his disciples to the lake, and a large crowd followed. Because of the crowd he told his disciples to have a small boat ready for him, to keep the people from crowding him. For he had healed many, so that those with diseases were pushing forward to touch him. Whenever the evil spirits saw him, they fell down before him and cried out, "You are the Son of God." But he gave them strict orders not to tell who he was.

(MARK 3:7, 9–12)

THIS ACCOUNT serves as another summary passage of Jesus's ministry. The purpose for Mark using summaries like this is to demonstrate the fact that Jesus performed many more healings and exorcisms than are recorded. Mark has only selected "a few instances from Jesus' career to report in detail."[1] This summary also serves to let the reader know that Jesus's popularity and reputation extended far beyond the geographic location where He lived and ministered. People came from all over the region to hear Him. Jesus had become very popular with the sick and poor.[2]

Mark emphasizes that the crowd was pushing in around Jesus trying to get near Him. Instead of waiting on Him to touch *them*, they try and force their way close enough to touch *Him*. Later, Mark will provide an example of someone who pushed through the crowd to touch Jesus. Here, the crowd was evidently pushing and shoving and causing such a commotion that He had a boat on standby if things got out of control. We also know that Jesus often used a boat anchored just offshore as a platform that He taught from.

1. Achtemeier, *Mark*, 29.
2. Juel, *Mark*, 58.

This passage also refers to Jesus performing exorcisms. This was evidently a very important part of Jesus's ministry. As with the healings, Mark only picks a few accounts of Jesus casting out demons to describe in detail. As in the first account that we examined in Mark 1:21-28, the demons recognize Jesus and scream out, "You are the Son of God." Jesus orders the evil spirits to be quiet.

There are probably four main reasons that Jesus refuses to allow the demons to identify Him.[3] The first is the fact that it is not fitting for filthy and corrupt spirits to proclaim the identity and work of the Holy Son of God. A second reason is because the title "the Son of God" implied that Jesus was the Messiah. The concept of Messiah, however, was understood in a nationalistic sense. He would be someone who would deliver them from the bondage of Roman rule and reestablish the national kingdom of Israel. Jesus understanding of His Messianic mission was drastically different from this. He understood that He had to suffer and die for the sins of mankind.

The third reason that Jesus did not allow the evil spirits to identify Him was the fact that the religious leaders were telling the people that Jesus and the demons were working together. If Jesus allowed Himself to be proclaimed as the Son of God by the demons, this would seem to confirm the allegations of the religious authorities. Jesus will later refute this charge by saying, "How can Satan drive out Satan? If a kingdom is divided against itself, that kingdom cannot stand. If a house is divided against itself, that house cannot stand. And if Satan opposes himself and is divided, he cannot stand; his end has come."[4]

A fourth reason that Jesus did not allow the demons to speak was that the title, "The Son of God," can only truly be understood in the light of Jesus's death and resurrection. As we will see, it will only be at the crucifixion that a human being will acknowledge Jesus as the Son of God. The irony that Mark brings out here and in Mark 3:22, is that the demons do understand the reality of who Jesus is while the religious leaders accuse Jesus of being demon possessed Himself!

---

3. Hendriksen, *Mark*, 121-22. See also Brooks, *Mark*, 70.
4. Mark 3:24-26.

10

Sleeping through the Storm

> *That day when evening came, he said to his disciples, "Let us go to the other side." Leaving the crowd behind, they took him along, just as he was, in the boat. There were also other boats with him. A furious squall came up, and the waves broke over the boat, so that it was nearly swamped. Jesus was in the stern, sleeping on a cushion. The disciples woke him and said to him, "Teacher, don't you care if we drown?" He got up, rebuked the wind and said to the waves, "Quiet! Be still!" Then the wind died down and it was completely calm. He said to his disciples, "Why are you so afraid? Do you still have no faith?" They were terrified and asked each other, "Who is this? Even the wind and the waves obey him?"*
>
> (MARK 4:35–41)

THIS MIRACLE is the first of several "nature" miracles that Mark records. Jesus has just finished teaching all day. It was indicated earlier that He probably spent part of the day teaching while sitting in a boat anchored just off shore. Now He is ready to cross the lake and instructs His disciples to take Him to the other side. Mark records that they left the crowd behind but says that as they started across the lake, "There were also other boats with him." There is no indication that all twelve of the disciples were in the boat with Jesus. If they were not, these other boats could be referring to the rest of the disciples and possibly others of Jesus's followers. It could also be the case that people from the crowd were following behind in these other boats to see where Jesus was going and what He was going to do next.

Without much other preamble, Mark says that a terrible storm came up suddenly, complete with vicious winds and waves that were breaking over the sides of the boat. The Sea of Galilee has long been infamous for these sudden squalls. "Surrounded by mountains at most points, the lake swirls violently when a strong wind enters."[1] For anyone who has ever been caught in a storm in a small or even medium sized boat, it is easy to imagine the fear that the disciples felt. It is interesting to note, however, that most of Jesus's disciples were experienced boatmen. They were career fishermen and had probably been through a few storms. The fact that these experienced fishermen were scared seems to point to the severity of the storm. As English notes, "it is usually the experts who recognize the need to panic!"[2]

By way of contrast, Jesus is sleeping soundly in the stern of the ship. It is evident that He is exhausted. Teaching all day has taken its toll on Him. This is a beautiful snapshot of Jesus's humanity. He is so tired that He is sleeping through this terrible storm. Mark's picture of Jesus's physical exhaustion will also provide a interesting contrast when He confronts the storm later.

The disciples' fear finally became so great, that they awoke Jesus, and with more than a little petulance ask, "Teacher, don't you care if we drown?" Granted, it was their fear that caused them use a reproachful tone with Jesus. One senses the desperation that the disciples must have been feeling, however, for the fishermen to ask the carpenter to do something!

One wonders what the disciples expected Jesus to do. Maybe they wanted an extra set of hands bailing water out of the boat. Maybe they needed some help keeping the boat on course in the pounding waves. Or maybe, the disciples, even with their imperfect understanding of Who Jesus was, felt that if He was awake, He could do something to help or protect them.

After being wakened, Jesus got up and confronted the storm. He spoke to the storm as if it were a person, "Quiet! Be still!" In fact the language that Jesus uses is similar to the way in which He spoke to the demon possessed man He encountered in the Capernaum synagogue. The word He uses here for "be still" literally means to "be muzzled."[3] The result is that the winds and the sea obey, just as the demons do.

---

1. Brooks, *Mark*, 87. See also Hendriksen, *Mark*, 176–77.
2. English, *The Message of Mark*, 106.
3. John, *The Meaning*, 73.

Not only do the winds and sea obey, but they do it instantly. In a moment, the winds died down and the surface of the sea became "completely calm." The sea became as smooth as glass. The Psalmist wrote:

> For he spoke and stirred up a tempest that lifted high the waves. They mounted up to the heavens and went down to the depths; in their peril their courage melted away. They reeled and staggered like drunken men; they were at their wits end. Then they cried out to the Lord in their trouble, and he brought them out of their distress. *He stilled the storm to a whisper; the waves of the sea were hushed.* They were glad when it grew calm, and he guided them to their desired haven.[4] (my italics)

This Psalm seems to prophetically capture this incident on the Sea of Galilee. Jesus is shown here exercising divine authority. It is not "just the portrait of a wonder-worker; it is the story of a divine revelation."[5] God's power over nature is present in Jesus, just as it was at creation. "That Jesus shares the power of God as the Lord of the mysteries of creation is the main teaching of [this story]."[6]

This miracle provides the clearest revelation of Who Jesus is in Mark's Gospel up to this point. The disciples, however, still do not seem to have a clear grasp of Jesus's divinity. They ask, "Who is this? Even the wind and the waves obey him!" The disciples actually appear to be more frightened over what they had seen Jesus do to the storm than they had been of the storm itself. Mark records that, "They were terrified" after Jesus had exercised authority over the elements. Translated literally, Mark says that the disciples "feared a great fear." They have seen Jesus exercise authority over crowds, sickness, disease, and evil spirits.[7] This display by Jesus is beyond anything that they could imagine.

Jesus recognizes the disciples' fear and addresses it. "Why are you so afraid?" Note, He does not ask them, "Why were you so afraid?" As we just mentioned, they are more afraid now by the realization that they are confronting something that they do not understand. Jesus

---

4. Psalm 107: 25–30.
5. Fuller, *Interpreting*, 54.
6. Richardson, *The Miracle Stories*, 90.
7. Hendriksen, *Mark*, 180.

continues, "Do you still have no faith?" In asking if they "still" have no faith, Jesus is gently rebuking the disciples' unbelief. After all they have seen Him do, and all they have heard Him teach, they should have a better grasp of Who He is. This miracle should have been a final piece to the puzzle of Jesus's identity.

One of the small details that Mark includes in his account of this miracle is the mention of the other boats that were with Jesus and His disciples on the lake. In calming the storm, Jesus demonstrated His mercy on a scale beyond just saving His disciples.[8] This miracle had an impact on the other people in the other boats as well.

A last aspect of this miracle that will be discussed is the how this miracle has been interpreted in Church history. The boat has often been seen as a figure of the Church being buffeted by the waves and winds of persecution and temptation.[9] It might seem that Jesus is asleep and does not care about what His people are going through. In reality, however, He "awakens" at just the right time and rebukes the storm.

On a personal level, this is a question that we must all come face to face with at some time: "Teacher, don't you care if we drown?" Does Jesus care if we are battling sickness? Does Jesus care if we lose our job? Does Jesus care if our teenager storms out of the house telling us that they hate us? Does Jesus care if our marriage breaks up? While we know from the Scriptures that the answer to each of these questions is a resounding "yes," each of us has to experience God's grace and concern for ourselves. A true faith is a tested faith.

---

8. Cole, *Mark*, 154.
9. Richardson, *The Miracle Stories*, 92–93.

11

The Gerasene Demoniac

They went across the lake to the region of the Gerasenes. When Jesus got out of the boat, a man with an evil spirit came from the tombs to meet him. This man lived in the tombs, and no one could bind him any more, not even with a chain. For he had often been chained hand and foot, but he tore the chains apart and broke the irons on his feet. No one was strong enough to subdue him. Night and day among the tombs and in the hills he would cry out and cut himself with stones. When he saw Jesus from a distance, he ran and fell on his knees in front of him. He shouted at the top of his voice, "What do you want with me, Jesus, Son of the Most High God? Swear to God that you won't torture me!" For Jesus had said to him, "Come out of this man, you evil spirit!" Then Jesus asked him, "What is your name?" "My name is Legion," he replied, "for we are many." And he begged Jesus again and again not to send them out of the area. A large herd of pigs was feeding on the nearby hillside. The demons begged Jesus, "Send us among the pigs; allow us to go into them." He gave them permission, and the evil spirits came out and went into the pigs. The herd, about two thousand in number, rushed down the steep bank into the lake and were drowned. Those tending the pigs ran off and reported this in the town and countryside, and the people went out to see what had happened. When they came to Jesus, they saw the man who had been possessed by the legion of demons, sitting there, dressed and in his right mind; and they were afraid. Those who had seen it told the people what had happened to the demon-possessed man—and told about the pigs as well. Then the people began to plead with Jesus to leave their region. As Jesus was getting into the boat, the man who had been demon-pos-

> *sessed begged to go with him. Jesus did not let him, but said, "Go home to your family and tell them how much the Lord has done for you, and how he has had mercy on you." So the man went away and began to tell in the Decapolis how much Jesus had done for him. And all the people were amazed.*
>
> (MARK 5:1–20)

THIS STORY provides a very detailed account of Jesus interacting with a severe demoniac. Mark writes that this encounter took place after Jesus and His disciples had crossed the lake to "the region of the Gerasenes." There is some conflict about the actual location that is being discussed here. That argument is beyond the scope of this study. There are several facts about the location that seem to be clear, however. First of all, this appears to be Jesus' first trip outside of Palestine.[1] A second fact is that the people in this region kept pigs indicating that they were probably not Jewish. A third fact is that there was also a cemetery close by. The pigs and the cemetery both would indicate impurity for a good Jew. As Juel puts it, "The whole land is taboo for Jews, but as has been customary, Jesus ventures precisely into such forbidden territory."[2]

Mark provides a vivid description of the tormented man. He lived outside of society by himself among the tombs. The local people had tried to restrain him, probably as much for their own peace of mind as for the man's protection. The evil spirits evidently provided him with supernatural strength because Mark notes that "he tore the chains apart and broke the irons on his feet." It is possible that he was even wearing the remains of his bonds on his wrists or feet when he encountered Jesus.

While living by himself, Mark notes that "he would cry out and cut himself with stones." He was obviously a danger to himself and as mentioned, this was probably one of the reasons that people tried to restrain him. Whether or not the demon possessed man was a danger to anyone else is not really clear, but it is easy to imagine how anyone living nearby would feel if they had to listen to him crying out in the

---

1. Brooks, *Mark*, 89.
2. Juel, *Mark*, 79.

middle of the night! The screams of a tormented man would have made sleep difficult

While I was a missionary in Ghana, West Africa, there were numerous occasions that I observed obviously disturbed individuals out walking around. Most were clothed in rags but occasionally they would be completely nude as they wandered around. People always went out of their way to avoid the "mad" men. I would guess that many of these people suffered from some type of mental illness but demonic oppression certainly was behind some of these cases. I know of one occasion in which one of these "mad" men wandered into an open air evangelistic meeting that an American friend of mine was preaching at. Within just a few moments of hearing the Word of God preached, the demons in the man began manifesting physically. The man became so disruptive that my friend had to stop preaching and deal with the demon possessed man. After a few minutes of intense prayer, the man was set free and had committed his life to Christ. Someone in the audience gave him something to put on over his nakedness. My friend later told me this incident reminded him of this story in Mark. The African man was now seated quietly, clothed, and in his right mind!

There is no indication here in Mark as to how long this man has been in this condition. One gets the sense that it has been for some time. The tormented man does not waste any time, however, in confronting Jesus. He was just getting out of the boat when the demoniac came running up to Him and fell on his knees. Some have translated this to say that "he ran and worshipped him."[3] This really does not capture the essence of what is happening here. Neither the man, nor the demons are worshipping Jesus. Rather, the demons are kneeling as an act of submission.[4] They recognize in Jesus One who has authority to drive them out. It is interesting that the tormented man runs towards Jesus instead of running away from Him. We would expect him to try and get as far away from Jesus as possible. Instead, he "is irresistibly drawn to Jesus."[5] Even in his state of bondage and torment, the man perceived that Jesus alone had the power to heal him.

---

3. KJV is one example.

4. Juel, ibid.

5. English, *The Message of Mark*, 109. See also Spell, *Peter and Paul*, 150–51.

MIRACLES IN MARK

Jesus immediately perceived the demonic activity and evidently began speaking to the demons as the man was running up to Him. Jesus said, "Come out of this man, you evil spirit!" Instead of coming out right away, however, the demons speak through their captive, "What do you want with me, Jesus, Son of the Most High God? Swear to God that you won't torture me!"

Jesus then asks the demons for their name. The response is, "My name is Legion, for we are many." There was a strong belief in the ancient world that if you knew someone's name, you had some measure of control over them.[6] This may be why the demons addressed Jesus by name. Obviously, this had no effect on Jesus and He commanded authority over the demons, whether He had their name or not. The demon here seems to be bragging about their strength. A "legion" in the Roman army represents around 6000 soldiers. This does not mean that that the man was possessed by 6000 demons. At the same time, the demon seems to be saying to Jesus, "we are a strong force to be reckoned with." The Bible does seem to indicate different levels of demonization.[7] Jesus is said to have cast seven demons out of Mary Magdalene.[8] This man seems to provide an example of severe bondage to many evil spirits.

There is no question that the demons understand that Jesus does have the authority to cast them out. The unclean spirits then began to bargain with Jesus. They do not want to leave the area. They feel comfortable there. This "is the terrain of tombs, skeletons, desertion, death, and destruction."[9] They begged Jesus, "Send us among the pigs; allow us to go into them." Jesus gives them permission and they enter the pigs. The entire herd of 2000 pigs then goes rushing down the steep bank into the lake where they drowned. The fate of the demons is unclear but the implication is that they are destroyed along with the pigs in the lake.[10]

Why did Jesus allow the demons to go into the pigs? This question has been long debated. Why would Jesus knowingly destroy someone's private property? This question, however, comes from a

6. John, *The Meaning*, 90.
7. Cole, *Mark*, 158.
8. Mark 16:9.
9. Hendriksen, *Mark*, 192.
10. Juel, *Mark*, 80.

modern point-of-view. The original audience would have thought nothing about this. Pigs were regarded as unclean and their destruction was acceptable. Juel even finds humor in the situation as Jesus uses the unclean pigs as an instrument "by which the unclean spirits are cleansed."[11]

Another possible reason that Jesus allows the spirits to go into the pigs is that in doing so, it provides a sort of spiritual safety valve to protect the possessed man.[12] Because there appear to be so many unclean spirits at work in this man, Jesus may have been protecting him by transferring them into the pigs. In the exorcism story recorded in Mark 9:14–29, it appears that the demons did great violence to the boy as Jesus cast them out. This story will be discussed in detail later, but it should be noted that here, when Jesus allows the demons to go into the pigs there are no recorded convulsions, shakings, etc.

The next aspect of this story is the interaction between the local people and Jesus. Those who were tending the sheep ran off and told the townspeople what had happened. A group of local residents then came to investigate. When they got there they found the man who had been demon possessed, sitting with Jesus, clothed, and in his right mind. At this point, we might expect an outpouring of appreciation from the people. The formerly demon possessed man provides a powerful testimony for them to see.[13] All would have known the story of the troubled man that they could hear screaming on quiet nights. Some in the crowd would have been the ones who had bound the possessed man with chains in an attempt to restrain him.

We might also expect an outburst of faith from the local people as they see the miracle that has been performed on this man.[14] We might expect them to gather their sick and bring them to Jesus. We might expect them to ask Jesus to stay for a while in their region. Instead of going to faith, however, they went to fear. These people were evidently superstitious and they were terrified of anyone who

---

11. Ibid. Juel goes on to point out that, "The destruction of the army of demons and the salvation of a human life are considered worth a herd of swine—at least by the author and his readers."

12. Cole, *Mark*, 157.

13. Hurtado, *Mark*, 84.

14. English, *The Message of Mark*, 111.

possessed the kind of power that Jesus obviously had.[15] The people are more afraid of Jesus than they were of the man in his demon possessed state. They could tolerate him because he could be relegated to the outskirts of society among the tombs.[16] Jesus, in the same way that He trampled on the Jewish norms, refuses to accept the status quo among the Gentiles as well. "He transgresses the boundaries and rescues those beyond help."[17]

Instead of welcoming Jesus, the people beg Him to leave. One gets the feeling, however, that Jesus's mission here was accomplished. This tormented man was the reason that Jesus crossed the lake with His disciples. In Luke 19:10, Jesus said, "For the Son of Man came to seek and to save what was lost." The story of this man's deliverance and subsequent salvation is an incredible picture of God's grace and shows His love for the individual.

The story of this man's healing provides a beautiful comparison with the previous story of Jesus's calming of the storm. There, Jesus spoke to the violent wind and waves calming them. The result was that, "the wind died down and it was completely calm." Here, the man whose life had been wracked by the storm of demon possession is now sitting quietly at Jesus's feet. The demons are gone and the man is experiencing true peace for the first time in his life.

The story opens with Jesus getting out of a boat. It closes as He is getting back into it. The man that Jesus had set free begs to accompany Him. Jesus refuses His request but commissions him instead: "Go home to your family and tell them how much the Lord has done for you, and how he has had mercy on you." Why would Jesus command this man to "go and tell" after ordering others to be silent after being healed or delivered? The most likely answer is that this incident took place in Gentile territory. There are not going to be the presuppositions about the Messiah here that there would be in Israel. The Gentiles would be free to hear the message about Jesus without any of the preconceived ideas that the Jews had. Jesus's commissioning of the man also foreshadowed a time when the Gospel would be preached to all the nations. A last reason for Jesus sending the man out to preach

---

15. Brooks, *Mark*, 91.
16. Juel, *Mark*, 81.
17. Ibid.

The Gerasene Demoniac

is because Jesus, Himself, was asked to leave the area. The man is now Jesus's representative to the region. We might think that his understanding of the Gospel was inadequate, yet he had experienced the power of God at a level that none of Jesus's disciples had yet and he embraced his mission with enthusiasm, telling "how much Jesus had done for him." The result was that "all the people were amazed."

12

Touching Jesus in the Crowd

A large crowd followed and pressed around him. And a woman was there who had been subject to bleeding for twelve years. She had suffered a great deal under the care of many doctors and had spent all she had, yet instead of getting better she grew worse. When she heard about Jesus, she came up behind him in the crowd and touched his cloak, because she thought, "If I just touch his clothes, I will be healed." Immediately, her bleeding stopped and she felt in her body that she was freed from her suffering. At once Jesus realized that power had gone out from him. He turned around in the crowd and asked, "Who touched my clothes?" "You see the people crowding against you," his disciples answered, "and yet you can ask, 'Who touched me?'" But Jesus kept looking around to see who had done it. Then the woman, knowing what had happened to her, came and fell at his feet and, trembling with fear, told him the whole truth. He said to her, "Daughter, your faith has healed you. Go in peace and be freed from your suffering."

(Mark 5:24–34)

This story actually takes place in the middle of another miracle story that will be discussed in the next chapter. Jesus was in the midst of a throng of people as He made His way to the house of a synagogue ruler. The snapshot we see is of Jesus in the middle of a swirling crowd all pressing in around Him. Schmidt translates it, "And a large crowd started following and shoving against him."[1]

Mark's description of the woman puts her in sharp contrast with Jairus, the synagogue ruler. As a woman, she already occupies

---

1. Schmidt, *The Gospel of Mark*, 75.

a low place in Palestinian society. Her sickness compounds matters. The woman "had been subject to bleeding for twelve years." John describes her condition as "some kind of menstrual disorder that had proved incurable by medical means."[2] Depending on the severity of the bleeding, this was likely a life threatening sickness. She had been to many doctors but instead of getting better, she had only grown worse. Aside from the health issues, this type of sickness rendered her ritually impure. For twelve years, she has been regarded as unclean, and like the leper that Jesus healed earlier, the woman has essentially become a societal outcast. This woman had, in fact, lost her health, her wealth, and her place in society and the religious community.[3]

This unnamed woman, like so many other people that Mark discusses, had heard about Jesus. What she had heard had generated enough hope and faith in her that she was willing to sneak up behind Jesus in the crowd and touch his cloak. She felt, "If I just touch his clothes, I will be healed." It was a common belief in the ancient world that the clothes of a healer had healing power themselves. This was seen in Acts 19 where sweat rags that Paul had used were taken and applied to the sick or demon possessed with good results.[4]

This was the perfect setting for her plan. The tumultuous crowd would provide an excellent cover for her. She could squeeze in with everyone else that was pressing against Jesus, touch His cloak, and then slip away unnoticed. She did not want to risk "the consequences of defiling a holy man by touching him in her unclean state."[5] She also did not want to risk the embarrassment of disclosure or the hostility of the crowd.

As she pressed into the mix of people thronging around Jesus, she was able to reach out and touch his cloak. Mark tells us that the bleeding stopped immediately "and she felt in her body that she was freed from her suffering." Before she could slip away, however, Jesus stopped moving. Mark paints a humorous picture as Jesus, at the middle of the crowd, stops, forcing everyone else to stop as well. Jesus

---

2. John, *The Meaning*, 100.
3. Hendriksen, *Mark*, 205-206.
4. For a discussion of this in Acts, see Spell, *Peter and Paul*, 152-54.
5. Brooks, *Mark*, 96.

MIRACLES IN MARK

had felt the "touch" of the woman and "realized that power had gone out from him."[6]

Jesus asked the crowd of people around Him, "Who touched my clothes?" Before anyone can answer, the disciples (Luke specifies that it was Peter) incredulously say, "You see the people crowding against you and yet you can ask, 'Who touched me?'" The disciples' response to Jesus here is sarcastic, disrespectful and rude. Mark alone among the Gospels conveys the petulant attitude of the disciples towards Jesus. The fact that they do not yet know what has happened is understandable. This is a chaotic scene! What is amazing is the fact that after all they have seen Him do the disciples are still questioning Jesus instead of watching, waiting and seeing what He is up to at any particular moment.

Mark's attention now shifts back to the healed woman. When she realizes that she cannot get away undetected she, "came and fell at his feet and, trembling with fear, told him the whole truth." Her fear was probably the result of a couple of different factors. First of all, she could have been expecting a rebuke from Jesus for touching Him while she was unclean.[7] Instead of rebuking her, Jesus commends her faith, "Daughter, your faith has healed you. Go in peace and be freed from your suffering." So, while "Jewish ritual requirement forbade her to touch any holy thing, she is delivered precisely by touching Jesus, the Son of God!"[8]

A second reason for her fear was likely the idea of being exposed before the crowd. Her illness was one that would have been embarrassing and not the kind of thing that she would want everyone to know about. She had also shown a measure of impropriety in the way that she approached Jesus. Her confession of what had happened, however, was the thing that probably healed her spirit as well. She had touched Jesus and been healed. Now Jesus speaks to her and affirms her faith. When Jesus told her, "Your faith has healed you," He was speaking of the whole person. The word for "healed" that is used here is the perfect tense of the Greek verb, *sōzō*, and can be defined "to save,"[9] as well as

---

6. Cole, *Mark*, 161. Cole notes that healings such as this may have cost Jesus spiritual energy for there are many times when He pulls away from the masses for recuperation and prayer.

7. Brooks, ibid.

8. Hurtado, *Mark*, 88.

9. Brooks, ibid. See also John, *The Meaning*, 103.

"to heal." The KJV translates this as "Thy faith hath made thee whole." This seems to be what Jesus is telling her. Her faith had not only healed her, it had also saved her and made her whole.

This miracle provides a beautiful picture of how faith works. Many people may throng around Jesus but not know anything of His incredible power. It is "only those who, conscious of their own unworthiness, come to Him in faith, are made whole."[10] This woman came to Jesus seeking a healing. She leaves a new creature and restored to participation in the community again.

---

10. Richardson, *The Miracle Stories*, 61.

13

Waking up a Little Girl

While he was by the lake, one of the synagogue rulers named Jairus, came there. Seeing Jesus, he fell at his feet and pleaded earnestly with him, "My little daughter is dying. Please come and put your hands on her so that she will be healed and live." So Jesus went with him . . . While Jesus was still speaking, some men came from the house of Jairus, the synagogue ruler. "Your daughter is dead," they said. "Why bother the teacher any more?" Ignoring what they said, Jesus told the synagogue ruler, "Don't be afraid; just believe." He did not let anyone follow him except Peter, James and John the brother of James. When they came to the home of the synagogue ruler, Jesus saw a commotion, with people crying and wailing loudly. He went in and said to them, "Why all this commotion and wailing? The child is not dead but asleep." But they laughed at him. After he put them all out, he took the child's father and mother and the disciples who were with him, and went in where the child was. He took her by the hand and said to her, "Talitha koum!" (which means, "Little girl, I say to you, get up!"). Immediately the girl stood up and walked around (she was twelve years old). At this they were completely astonished. He gave strict orders not to let anyone know about this, and told them to give her something to eat.

(MARK 5:21–24, 35–43)

THIS MIRACLE is often seen as the climax to the miracles that Mark presents in his Gospel. It gains added impact by being paired with the healing of the woman with the bleeding issue. This is the first account in Mark in which Jesus is approached by a member of the reli-

Waking up a Little Girl

gious establishment in a respectful and interested way.[1] Granted, he is seeking something from Jesus and it is possible that Jesus was his last option. It cannot be denied, however, that when the synagogue ruler, Jairus, does approach Jesus, it is with sincerity and humility.

We are not told how Jairus had heard about Jesus. It is clear that Jesus's reputation was pretty well established by this point. A likely scenario is that Jairus was the ruler of the synagogue that Jesus regularly attended in Capernaum.[2] If this is the case, he had seen Jesus in action and knew He would be able to help his daughter. It appears that Jairus was looking for Jesus when he approached Him and found Him by the lake. One can wonder how long he had been looking for the Teacher. Any parent has some understanding of how Jairus felt. When our child is sick with a fever or a virus and nothing seems to be working, a variety of emotions can surge through us: desperation, frustration, anger, helplessness. Would Jairus, a respected member of the religious establishment that openly opposed Jesus, have requested healing from Jesus for himself? Probably not but it is an interesting question. Again, those of us who are parents understand that our children will cause us to take measures that we would not normally take.

When Jairus located Jesus, he put all of his respectability aside and fell at Jesus's feet and "pleaded earnestly with him, '"My little daughter is dying. Please come and put your hands on her so that she will be healed and live."' While Jairus's desperation is evident, so is his faith. He has heard or seen enough of Jesus to know that He could heal his daughter. At this point in the story, Jesus has not said anything. Mark just tells us, "So Jesus went with him."

As was discussed in the previous chapter, the procession to Jairus's house was interrupted by the woman with the hemorrhage. This stopped them for a few minutes as Jesus dealt with her. While Jesus is interacting with the healed woman, Jairus is in the shadows. All the attention is on Jesus and the woman who has experienced the miracle. It is easy to imagine how the delay would have affected Jairus. Every moment was crucial. His daughter was very sick. He knew that her life was on the line. Jesus had inspired hope in Jairus as He started with him to his home, but now they are delayed as Jesus talks with a woman, in public, who has confessed the fact that she was ritually

1. Juel, *Mark*, 82.
2. Hendriksen, *Mark*, 203.

unclean. It is wonderful that she was healed, but this was not helping his daughter.

"While Jesus was still speaking, some men came from the house of Jairus." Did Jairus see them coming? Did he read the expression on their faces? Their message confirmed his worst fears, "Your daughter is dead," they said. "Why bother the teacher any more?" Jesus's delay may have been lifesaving for the woman but it was fatal for Jairus's child.[3] The men who bring Jairus the news show a tremendous lack of tact and compassion in the way that they deliver it. Their attitude could be related to their own feelings towards Jesus. If they were also a part of the religious establishment, they may have resented Jairus going to Jesus for help in the first place.[4] Jesus had been performing miracle after miracle among the common people and was winning a great following. What kind of impact would the healing of a synagogue ruler's daughter have? Now that she is dead, their concern is allayed. While this attitude is cruel beyond measure, I do not believe that it is a misrepresentation of the kind of anger and hatred that Jesus's actions produced in people.

For the first time in this story, Jesus speaks to Jairus, "Don't be afraid; just believe." Jairus has just observed the power of having faith in Jesus in the woman that was healed. Jesus now calls on Jairus to exercise such faith.[5] The situation truly looks hopeless. With Jesus, however, "There are possibilities even where hope appears to be lost."[6] Jesus does not tell Jairus how this is going to end. He just encourages him to have faith. While despair might be a natural human emotion at such a time, Jesus urges Jairus to trust Him. He trusted Jesus before his daughter died. Now He urges him to continue trusting Him.

At this point, Jesus takes control over the noisy crowd. "He did not let anyone follow him except Peter, James, and John, the brother of James." We can easily understand Jesus dismissing the crowd. Why, though, would He also dismiss the majority of His disciples? One possibility is that Jesus left the nine disciples behind to restrain the crowd as Jesus, Jairus, Peter, James, and John slipped away to Jairus's home.

---

3. Juel, *Mark*, 84.
4. Brooks, *Mark*, 94.
5. Gundry, *Survey*, 139.
6. Juel, *Mark*, 85.

Waking up a Little Girl

Another reason that Jesus only took Peter, James, and John with Him is that they seem to represent the inner circle of the disciples.[7] These are also the ones that will witness the Transfiguration, hear Jesus teaching on the end times (along with Andrew), and accompany Him while He prayed in Gethsemane. These three, in spite of their imperfections and weaknesses probably represent the best of the Twelve up to that point. Peter, John, and James (until his martyrdom) will emerge as the leaders of the early Church.

When the group arrives at Jairus's house, they are confronted by another crowd and more noise and confusion. The crowd is "crying and wailing loudly." The ruler of the synagogue was an important person so the crowd of mourners was evidently larger than usual. Whether or not these were "professional mourners" really does not matter. A large group of people were creating quite a scene as Jesus arrived!

Jesus spoke to the crowd of mourners and said, "Why all this commotion and wailing? The child is not dead but asleep." The verb "to sleep" is used metaphorically in several other places in the New Testament to refer to death.[8] Jesus saw death from a divine perspective. He knew what He was going to do. The mourners sorrow quickly changed to laughter at Jesus's statement leading the reader to conclude that their grief was not genuine, or at least not very deep.[9]

Jesus quickly cast the mourners out of the house. Again, He has thinned the group out. Jesus has created an environment of faith. This is not a place for doubt. The mourners were expelled from the house because of their unbelief. He took the father and mother, along with his three disciples and went into the room where the young girl lay dead.

Jairus had initially approached Jesus and asked Him to come and lay His hands on his daughter so that she would, "be healed and live." Now, Jesus does just that. He takes the child by the hand and says, "Little girl, I say to you, get up!" She immediately got up and started walking around. There has been much discussion of Jesus's use of the Aramaic phrase, "*Talitha koum.*" The most probable reason for Mark's inclusion of this phrase is that Jesus used the same phrase the girl's mother would have used to wake her up in the mornings. Mark in-

7. Ibid. "If the Twelve represent an inner circle of insiders, Peter, James, and John represent the innermost circle."

8. Brooks, ibid, See John 11:11; 1 Corinthians 15:18; 1 Thessalonians 4:13.

9. Cole, *Mark,* 164.

MIRACLES IN MARK

cluded the Aramaic phrases for his Greek readers to get the flavor of the language that Jesus spoke.

The reaction of the parents (and probably the disciples as well!) was complete astonishment. It is easy to imagine the feelings of joy, relief, gratitude, and appreciation that these parents felt towards Jesus. The parents were instructed to give their daughter something to eat. This command was actually a proof that she really was alive. Ghosts or spirits do not eat.[10] This is also a practical command. Because of her sickness, the girl may not have eaten for some time. The food would build her strength back up.[11]

An interesting point that should be noted is the fact that, once again, Jesus was made ritually unclean, this time by the touching of a corpse. This was of no consequence to Him. Rather, He understood that His touch brought life, healing, and cleansing.[12] He understood that the power of God in Him overcame any uncleanness or sickness that He might encounter. This explains why He was always ready to eat and drink with "tax collectors and sinners," those who were morally defiled.

A last point that will be mentioned in the discussion of this miracle is the fact that Jesus again commanded silence in regards to this miracle. "He gave strict orders not to let anyone know about this." How could a miracle of this magnitude be kept silent? Brooks sees this command as no more than the parents not revealing the details of the miracle until Jesus has had a chance to get away so that He would not have to contend with a boisterous crowd.[13] Mark has emphasized throughout his Gospel that Jesus did not want to be known primarily on the basis of His miracles.[14] He performed acts like this out of His love and compassion for people but understood how they could be misunderstood by those who did not see them through the eyes of faith.

---

10. Juel, *Mark*, 878.
11. Hendriksen, *Mark*, 215.
12. Cole, *Mark*, 165.
13. Brooks, Mark, 95.
14. Tannehill, "The Gospel," 72.

14

The Feeding of the 5,000

The disciples gathered around Jesus and reported to him all they had done and taught. Then, because so many people were coming and going that they did not even have a chance to eat, he said to them, "Come away by yourselves to a quiet place and get some rest." So they went away by themselves in a boat to a solitary place. But many who saw them leaving and recognized them and ran on foot from all the towns and got there ahead of them. When Jesus landed a saw a large crowd, he had compassion on them, because they were like sheep without a shepherd. So he began teaching them many things. By this time it was late in the day, so his disciples came to him. "This is a remote place," they said, "and it's already very late. Send the people away so they can go to the surrounding countryside and villages and buy themselves something to eat." But he answered, "You give them something to eat." They said to him, "That would take eight months of a man's wages! Are we to go and spend that much on bread and give it to them to eat?" "How many loaves do you have?" he asked. "Go and see." When they found out, they said, "Five—and two fish." Then Jesus directed them to have all the people sit down in groups of hundreds and fifties. Taking the five loaves and the two fish and looking up to heaven, he gave thanks and broke the loaves. Then he gave them to his disciples to set before the people. He also divided the two fish among them all. They all ate and were satisfied, and the disciples picked up twelve basketfuls of broken pieces of bread and fish. The number of the men who had eaten was five thousand.

(MARK 6:30–44)

MIRACLES IN MARK

THE FEEDING of the five thousand is the only miracle that is recorded in all four Gospels. This miracle is preceded by a discussion of the disciples talking to Jesus about the results of the mission that He had sent them on. Earlier in the chapter, Jesus had commissioned the disciples and sent them out. "Calling the Twelve to him, he sent them out two by two and gave them authority over evil spirits ... They went out and preached that people should repent. They drove out many demons and anointed many sick people with oil and healed them."[1]

This marks the first time that Jesus has sent the Twelve out on a mission of this nature. Up to this point in the narrative, the disciples have not distinguished themselves. They have not appeared to understand Jesus's teaching. They question Him and are argumentative. They still seem to struggle with trusting Him.[2] In spite of all they have seen Jesus do, the Twelve do not seem to even fully know Who He is. Despite these limitations, however, Jesus still sends the Twelve out to perform the same kind of ministry that He has been performing.

It appears that this was a successful mission. The disciples preached a message of repentance and saw many people healed and delivered from evil spirits. This preaching tour seems to be an important step of preparation in the lives of the men that will ultimately lead the Church after Jesus is gone. It is important to note that Jesus did not wait until His followers had the clear understanding that they gained after the resurrection before sending them out. It could be argued that their knowledge and understanding increased as they went and did the same kinds of things that Jesus had been doing: preaching, healing, and casting out demons.

After their return, the disciples appear anxious to tell Jesus the results of their mission. The crowd, however, interferes with the debriefing. The disciples were not even able to eat, Mark records. Jesus then attempted to take the disciples away by themselves to a solitary place for rest. When they arrived there, though, the crowd had observed where they were going or anticipated it and a multitude was waiting for them.

We do not know what the disciples' reaction was to this, but Jesus's reaction was one of compassion. As tired as He was, He looked on the multitudes as "sheep without a shepherd." These people were Jesus's

---

1. Mark 6:7, 12–13.
2. English, *The Message of Mark*, 125.

The Feeding of the 5,000

mission. This shepherd imagery was familiar in Hebrew tradition.[3] In Ezekiel 34:12 the prophet writes, "As a shepherd looks after his scattered flock when he is with them, so I will look after my sheep ... I will tend them in good pasture, and the mountain heights of Israel will be their grazing land."[4] Psalm 23 is another classic passage that discusses the relationship of the shepherd and his sheep. This miracle story here in Mark contains much more Old Testament imagery that will be examined.

After Jesus has taught the multitude until late in the day, the disciples approach Jesus and tell Him to send the crowd away so that they can go into the surrounding villages to buy themselves something to eat. It is unclear how much of Jesus's compassion for the crowd that the disciples share. Mark said that the multitude had kept the disciples from eating so they may be concerned about getting their own dinner.

Jesus, astoundingly, tells the disciples, "You give them something to eat." Jesus seems to want the disciples to take responsibility here and make something happen.[5] It is one thing to have a successful preaching tour in which people were healed and set free. Here, Jesus seems to want the Twelve to understand that ministry sometimes involves feeding hungry people. As they so often do, the disciples wonder what Jesus is asking of them. Does he want them to go and buy food for this entire group of over five thousand people? They reply that it would take over eight months wages if that is what Jesus wanted them to do.

Jesus then asks them how much food they have on hand. The disciples, still not sure what Jesus is going to do, come up with five small loaves of bread and two fish. Without any explanation, He then orders the disciples to seat the crowd in groups of hundreds and fifties.

Jesus took the five loaves and two fish and "looking up to heaven, gave thanks." He broke the loaves and started giving them out to his disciples to distribute to the crowd. "He also divided the two fish among them all." At some point between the blessing and the distribution, the food was multiplied. The result was that, "They all ate and were satisfied."

---

3. Juel, *Mark*, 96–97.
4. Ezekiel 34:12, 14.
5. Hendriksen, *Mark*, 252.

MIRACLES IN MARK

At least three clear Old Testament pictures come into play here. The first is that of God's provision in the wilderness for the Hebrews after the exodus from Egypt. There, God miraculously provided manna and quail from heaven. God also used Moses to provide drinking water for them from a rock. The second Old Testament picture involves Jesus's seating of the people in groups of fifties and hundreds. This appears to be a reference to Moses' organization of the Israelites in the wilderness.[6]

The third Old Testament picture that Mark seems to allude to here is that of Elisha the prophet. Elisha told his servant to give twenty loaves of bread to a group of one hundred men to eat. The servant questioned whether or not there would be enough. "Elisha answered, "Give it to the people to eat. For this is what the Lord says: 'They will eat and have some left over.'" Then he set it before them, and they ate and had some left over, according to the word of the Lord."[7]

By drawing on this Old Testament imagery, Mark appears to be pointing out that Jesus is the fulfillment of the Law and the Prophets.[8] Mark will emphasize this point in greater detail at the Transfiguration. For now, however, it is enough to see Jesus seemingly taking on the roles of Moses and Elisha as He feeds the multitude in this story.

Mark's representation of Jesus's feeding of the five thousand also shows a clear link with the Last Supper.[9] Mark uses similar verbs in describing the both events. On both occasions, Jesus took the bread, gave thanks, broke it, and gave it to His disciples. Obviously, Mark wrote post resurrection so the Last Supper would have actually served to clarify what Jesus was doing in this miracle. Also, looking post resurrection at this story, Mark understood the symbolism of this miracle and the Last Supper. "The feeding anticipates the messianic banquet at the end of the age. The kingdom is at hand. The miracle as such is not as important for Mark as what it reveals about Jesus."[10]

This miracle is full of symbolism and rich imagery. However, we must not make the mistake of forgetting the practical aspects of what

---

6. Hurtado, *Mark*, 100.
7. 2 Kings 4:42–44.
8. John, *The Meaning*, 62.
9. Juel, *Mark*, 98–99.
10. Brooks, *Mark*, 108.

Jesus did for this large group of people. Jesus fed over five thousand hungry people.[11] He had been feeding their spirits with His teaching all day, but Jesus also understood the importance of feeding their bodies.

Another practical aspect of this miracle was the fact that there were twelve baskets of leftovers, which the disciples picked up. This seems to indicate that there was enough for each disciple to have a basket. Jesus cared about the multitude as a shepherd looking after His sheep. Jesus also cared about His disciples, those who had given up everything to follow Him. In the midst of providing for the multitude, Jesus made sure that His disciples got their dinner as well. In fact, these leftovers would probably feed them for several days to come.

---

11. Cole, *Mark*, 178.

15

Walking on the Water

> *When evening came, the boat was in the middle of the lake, and he was alone on land. He saw the disciples straining at the oars, because the wind was against them. About the fourth watch of the night, he went to them, walking on the lake. He was about to pass by them, but when they saw him walking on the lake, they thought he was a ghost. They cried out, because they all saw him and were terrified. Immediately he spoke to them and said, "Take courage!" It is I. Don't be afraid." Then he climbed into the boat with them, and the wind died down. They were completely amazed, for they had not understood about the loaves; their hearts were hardened.*
>
> (MARK 6:47–52)

THIS MIRACLE takes place right after the feeding of the five thousand. Jesus made his disciples get into the boat and start back across the lake while He dismissed the crowd. We are not told how He was planning on getting across the lake Himself, although we will find that out later. After dismissing His disciples and the crowd, Jesus, "went up on a mountainside to pray."[1] This was His pattern. After periods of intense ministry, Jesus would often withdraw to pray and recharge His spiritual batteries.

As we observed from the story of Jesus calming the storm in Mark 4:35–41, the weather on the lake was subject to sudden changes. Mark notes that "the disciples were straining at the oars because the winds were against them." This does not seem to indicate a storm like

---

1. Mark 6:46.

Walking on the Water

they encountered before "but a tiring, continuous head wind, necessitating steady, back-breaking rowing."[2]

Mark further records that Jesus saw this from where He was at on land. This poses a problem for two reasons. The first is the fact that it was apparently dark. Even if there were a full moon over the lake it is unlikely that Jesus could have seen the disciples. This leads to the second problem with Jesus being able to see the disciples from where He was at. If they were in the middle of the lake, it is possible that they were three or four miles out from the shore.[3] At this distance, it would be difficult to see the disciples even during the day.

What then, does Mark mean by saying that Jesus "saw the disciples straining at the oars?" Mark seems to be indicating a miracle here saying that Jesus had knowledge of the disciples' situation.[4] In fact, by highlighting Jesus's supernatural knowledge, he is preparing us for the next part of this story in which Jesus is seen walking across the lake.

The fourth watch of the night would have been between three and six in the morning. At this time, "he went to them, walking on the lake. He was about to pass by them, but when they saw him walking on the lake, they thought he was a ghost." As in the story of Jesus calming the storm in Mark 4, the writer makes strong allusions to the Old Testament. Psalm 77:19 says, "Your path led through the sea, your way through the mighty waters, though your footprints were not seen." This passage refers to God's deliverance of the Hebrews when He parted the Red Sea. Job 9:8 alludes to God at creation, "He alone stretches out the heavens and treads on the waves of the sea."

While Mark's description of this miracle is unvarnished, he clearly expects the reader to understand it as a theophany or a Christophany. In the feeding of the multitude, Jesus was pictured as the new Moses, or even the new "shepherd-king like David."[5] In walking on the lake, Jesus is being described as Divine. Whereas in the account of the

---

2. Cole, *Mark*, 179.
3. Hendriksen, *Mark*, 258.
4. Brooks, *Mark*, 111.
5. Hurtado, *Mark*, 103.

calming of the storm Jesus showed His divine power by calming the waves, here He shows it by walking on them.[6]

Mark does not explain why Jesus was going to walk by the disciples. One possible reason is to illustrate "the mysterious behavior of a divine being."[7] Could Jesus have been "intending to parade his deity before them?"[8] God did this with Moses in Exodus 33:19–23. Another possible reason that He was going to bypass them could have been to test their faith.[9] How would they handle a difficult situation if Jesus was not with them? In the previous storm, the disciples felt that even though Jesus was in the boat with them, He did not care what happened to them. Had they learned from that experience?

Whatever the reason, it does not really matter because the disciples observed Jesus walking on the water and thought He was a ghost or *phantasma*. Did the disciples glimpse Jesus walking on the water as the moon came out from behind a cloud or was there something more illuminating Him? The word that is used here for "ghost" can refer to any kind of apparition, vision, or specter.[10] The root word carries the additional ideas of "to cause to appear, bring to light, to shine."[11] Another derivative word is *phanos*, which means "a torch, lantern, light."[12] Is it possible that the disciples saw Jesus as He radiated heavenly glory? If this is a theophany or Christophany, Jesus may have been manifesting the glory of God as He walked across the water, as He would do later on the Mountain of Transfiguration. If this was the case, Mark did not really emphasize it but it should not be ruled out.

At any rate, Jesus's appearance terrified the disciples and caused them to cry out. Anyone who has ever been startled so bad that they yelled or cried out involuntarily understands this response from the disciples. While most commentators criticize the disciples' reaction of being terrified, I cannot help but believe that their reaction was a nor-

---

6. Hendriksen, *Mark*, 260.
7. Fuller, *Interpreting*, 59.
8. Gundry, *Survey*, 141.
9. Cole, *Mark*, 180. See also English, *The Message of Mark*, 138.
10. Feyerabend, *Pocket Dictionary*, 400.
11. Moulton, *Lexicon*, 422.
12. Ibid.

mal one.[13] We do not expect to see a person walking across a lake in the middle of the night, especially if He appeared to be glowing. Even in the imagery of theophany, when God appeared in bodily form in the Old Testament, the typical initial reaction was often one of fear.[14]

Jesus spoke quickly to calm His followers' fears. Even Jesus's words, however, convey the language of divinity: "Take courage! It is I. Don't be afraid." Literally translated, this would read, "Take heart! *I am*. Be not afraid."[15] Jesus is clearly telling His followers Who He is. While we come to expect this kind of language in John's Gospel, it almost takes us by surprise here. It is pretty clear, though, that none of this registers with the disciples.

Jesus climbed into the boat and the wind immediately died down. Mark then provides us with an important insight about the disciples. He says, "They were completely amazed, for they had not understood about the loaves; their hearts were hardened." The disciples had only perceived the miraculous feeding as a miracle in which Jesus multiplied some food. What they did not perceive was Jesus's identity which the miracle pointed to. If they had, they would have recognized Him when He came walking to them on the lake.[16] This is not what we expect to hear. We expect to hear that the hearts of the religious leaders are hard. We do not expect to hear this about Jesus's own followers. At the same time, however, they are still Jesus's disciples and not His enemies. This is one of the ironies that Mark builds on. After all they have seen and experienced, the disciples are still not sure who Jesus is.[17]

---

13. Brooks, *Mark*, 112. "[T]he crying out, the terror, and the amazement are further indications of the disciples' unbelief and misunderstanding."
14. Exodus 3:6; Exodus 20:18–19; Judges 13:18–ff; Isaiah 6:5.
15. John, *The Meaning*, 77.
16. Brooks, *Mark*, ibid.
17. Ibid.

16

Healings at Gennesaret

When they had crossed over, they landed at Gennesaret and anchored there. As soon as they got out of the boat, people recognized Jesus. They ran throughout that whole region and carried the sick on mats to wherever they heard he was. And wherever he went- into villages, towns or countryside-they placed the sick in the marketplaces. They begged him to let them touch even the edge of his cloak, and all who touched him were healed.
(MARK 6:53–56)

THIS PASSAGE forms another summary passage that Mark uses to transition from one section of his narrative to another. The difference between this summary passage and the previous two (1:39; 3:7–12) is that this passage focuses on Jesus healing ministry. No mention is made of His teaching or casting out demons. These summaries again remind the reader that Jesus did much more than Mark was able to record.[1]

A couple of items from this summary deserve mentioning. First of all, the, "people recognized Jesus." Even though He often told recipients of healings or other miracles not to talk about it, word of His actions had gotten around. Word of His arrival caused a frenzy of activity as people thronged to see Him and to bring those who needed His healing touch.

Another interesting point is that "they placed the sick in the marketplaces." This seems to indicate that there were so many sick people being brought to Jesus, they had to use the largest open space in the villages. These were not small, isolated incidents of healing. Large numbers of people were experiencing the power of God. People

---

1. Achtemeier, *Mark*, 29.

were being brought to Jesus from all over the region. As they were healed and went back to their villages they took the message of Jesus back with them.

A last aspect of this narrative summary that warrants mention is the fact that the sick people were begging Jesus to touch the edge of His cloak, "and all who touched him were healed." This was how the woman with the hemorrhage was healed in the previous chapter. It seems clear that that account has been spread by word of mouth throughout the countryside because so many people ask if they can touch Him. Whether the people realized it or not, it was their faith in the One who wore the garment and not the garment itself that healed them.[2]

---

2. Cole, *Mark*, 181.

17

Feeding the Dogs under the Table

> *Jesus left that place and went to the vicinity of Tyre. He entered a house and did not want anyone to know it; yet he could not keep his presence secret. In fact, as soon as she heard about him, a woman whose little daughter was possessed by an evil spirit came and fell at his feet. The woman was a Greek, born in Syrian Phoenicia. She begged Jesus to drive the demon out of her daughter. "First let the children eat all they want," he told her, "for it is not right to take the children's bread and toss it to their dogs." "Yes, Lord," she replied, "but even the dogs under the table eat the children's crumbs." Then he told her, "For such a reply, you may go; the demon has left your daughter." She went home and found her child lying on the bed, and the demon gone.*
>
> (MARK 7:24–30)

THIS MIRACLE account starts with the report that Jesus went to Tyre. This was Gentile territory. This type of story leaves the reader wondering how many trips Jesus took like this outside of Israel. There is no indication given as to why Jesus ventured so far out of Israel. Perhaps He was looking for the solitude and rest that had eluded Him earlier[1]. He did not want anyone to know of His presence so it does not sound like He was there for a ministry trip.

Jesus's presence could not be kept secret, however, and He was approached by a woman who was identified as "a Greek, born in Syrian Phoenicia." It is unlikely that she was a Greek by nationality or by birth.[2] She was a Gentile, however, and was probably thoroughly Hellenized and spoke Greek when she came to Jesus. We again see how

1. Lane, *Mark*, 260.
2. Brooks, *Mark*, 121.

far Jesus's reputation had spread and how difficult it was for Him to maintain a low profile. It is also interesting to see how Mark highlights again, Jesus's interaction with a woman, this time a Gentile woman.

The reason that she seeks Jesus out is because her "little daughter was possessed by an evil spirit." This emphasis on her "little daughter" highlights how distraught the woman is. This is the first account in Mark where a child is said to be demon possessed. The idea of a child being demon possessed is very difficult and is worth commenting on. For those whose theology does not accept the idea of literal demon possession, it is easy to interpret this passage as Jesus healing an epileptic child, or some similar illness. As we have discussed previously, however, Mark (and the other Gospel writers as well) seems to mark a clear differentiation between sickness and demon possession.

If there is such a thing as demon possession, oppression, etc, how is it possible for a child be exposed to evil spirits? There are several likely ways this could happen. First of all, it could happen through pagan religious practices. Paul understood that the power behind the idols that pagans worshipped was demonic: ". . . the sacrifices of pagans are offered to demons, not to God, and I do not want you to be participants with demons."[3] We should not be surprised that a child that is dedicated to a pagan god at birth has to deal with demonic oppression later in life when they are exposed to the Christian message.

Another way that children can be exposed to demonic forces is through their parents. If the parents are participants in occult practices or pagan rituals, their children are going to be affected as well. Parents, who dabble in sorcery, witchcraft, idol worship, etc, are creating an environment in which their children become easy prey for demonic spirits.

A third way that children can be exposed to evil spirits is through abuse. Children who are traumatized at an early age, through no fault of their own, have areas of their mind opened that are not meant to be opened yet. This is especially true in the area of sexual abuse. This can create a doorway for demons to come in. This is not to say that every child that is abused struggles with demonic oppression. There are some, however, that do and find freedom when they commit their lives to Christ.

---

3. 1 Corinthians 10:20.

The first thing that the woman did when she found Jesus was to throw herself at His feet. This was an indication of both grief and reverence.[4] Over and over again, Mark shows people on their knees or prostrated before Jesus. The leper "begged him on his knees." The Gerasene demoniac "ran and fell on his knees in front of him." Jairus "fell at his feet" and pleaded with Jesus to come and heal his daughter. The woman who was healed of her bleeding "fell at his feet" after her healing was discovered.

The Gentile woman here then "begged Jesus to drive the demon out of her daughter." This is the same type of situation that Jesus has faced repeatedly in His ministry. People come to Jesus with a need and ask for His help. On every occasion that we have read of, Jesus has granted their request. Here, however, we see a different response from Jesus. There is no hint of political correctness in the way that Jesus answers the woman. He seems to be embracing the common prejudice that Jews had against the Gentiles. Jesus draws a stark contrast between the children (the Jews) and the dogs (the Gentiles). The word that Jesus uses here for "dogs" actually means "little dogs" or perhaps even "puppies." While this might be intended to soften its affect, there is still no escaping the insult that is given.

This comment by Jesus seems to contradict our view of His nature and personality. Jesus's words effectively exclude and insult the woman who is petitioning Him. The "kind and loving" Jesus that we expect appears to give way to someone who is harsh and insensitive.[5] To our modern sensibilities, Jesus's answer to the woman is completely unacceptable. In the first century, however, His comments are completely in line with contemporary Jewish thought. The Jews saw themselves as the children of God. They were the chosen people. They had the covenant, the promises and the Torah. The Gentiles, on the other hand, were routinely referred to as "dogs" in contemporary Jewish writings. This does not lessen the blow of Jesus's words. They still would have stung the hearer. What, then, was the woman's reaction to Jesus's apparent rebuff?

We might have expected her to leave after having been so insulted. Instead, she accepts what Jesus says but takes it one step farther. "Yes, Lord," she replied, but even the dogs under the table eat the

4. Brooks, *Mark*, 120.
5. Lane, *Mark*, 262.

children's crumbs." It does not have to be one or the other. If the dogs are eating the crumbs under the table, they are eating at the same time as the children.[6] The meal does not have to be interrupted for the dogs to eat. The woman's answer shows incredible insight and respect for Jesus. She refers to Him as "Lord." Her confidence in Jesus does not appear to be shaken.

Jesus then pronounces the healing of her daughter. "For such a reply, you may go; the demon has left your daughter." Jesus seems to have been testing the woman's faith by His aloofness and harshness. How bad did she want to see her daughter healed? Her humility and faith were seen in her acceptance of status as a "dog." She was the mother of a needy child, however, and she was going to do whatever she had to do to see her daughter healed.[7] The mother's social status was unimportant. What was important was seeing her child delivered. Her faith had initially been seen in her coming to Jesus in the first place. Her faith was further demonstrated by taking Jesus at His word. There is no indication that she asks Him to accompany her to where her daughter is. Instead, she accepts Jesus pronouncement of healing and goes home to find her daughter delivered from the demon.

This is not an easy story to read. It is difficult seeing Jesus act in a way that is not consistent with our view of Him. The story does, however, provide us with a reminder that Jesus's mission to the Gentiles was always secondary to His mission to the Jews.[8] In this miracle, though, we also see further foreshadowing of the day when the message will be preached "to all creation."[9]

One last aspect of this miracle needs to be mentioned. This is the first miracle that Mark provides in which Jesus heals someone from a distance. Jesus shows His power by speaking a word. The child was delivered without Jesus having to be there. In seeing this, the reader gets further confirmation of Jesus's divine power as He continues to do those things that only God can do.

---

6. Ibid, 263.
7. English, *The Message of Mark*, 149.
8. John, *The Meaning*, 112.
9. Mark 16:15.

18

Healing a Deaf Mute

Then Jesus left the vicinity of Tyre and went down through Sidon, down to the Sea of Galilee and into the region of the Decapolis. There some people brought to him a man who was deaf and could hardly talk, and they begged him to place his hand on the man. And after he took him aside, away from the crowd, Jesus put his fingers into the man's ears. Then he spit and touched the man's tongue. He looked up to heaven and with a deep sigh said to him, "Ephphatha!" (which means, "Be opened!") At this, the man's ears were opened, his tongue was loosened and he began to speak plainly. Jesus commanded them not to tell anyone. But the more he did so, the more they kept talking about it. People were overwhelmed with amazement. "He has done everything well," they said. "He even makes the deaf hear and the mute speak."

(MARK 7:31–37)

THIS MIRACLE, like the one preceding it, also takes place in Gentile territory. There is no indication in this story, though, that the subject of the healing is a Gentile. The Decapolis was last mentioned as the area that the Gerasenes demoniac had preached in after Jesus had delivered him. This region was also known for having numerous Jewish colonies.[1] It seems likely that this evangelistic activity coupled with Jesus's own increasing popularity had prepared the way for His ministry there.

This story starts off in a similar manner as the healing of the paralytic in 2:1–12 in the way that the man in need of healing was brought to Jesus by "some people," presumably friends. At least initially, it seems to be the faith of the friends that prompted this contact

---

1. Cole, *Mark*, 190.

Healing a Deaf Mute

with Jesus. Their request is that He, "place his hand on the man." There is no specific request for healing mentioned. It is possible that the friends brought the man to Jesus for a blessing. The laying on of hands was a Jewish custom normally used to convey a blessing.[2] In Jesus's ministry, however, the laying on of hands also came to be used as a way of conveying God's healing power.

In describing the man's condition, Mark says that he was "deaf and could hardly talk." The word that Mark uses here is, *mogilalos*, a rare word and only used in this passage in the New Testament. It refers to a speech impediment rather than someone who was born unable to speak.[3] This seems to imply that the man was not born deaf or else he probably would not have been able to speak at all. If he were born deaf, he would have no concept of language. He had become deaf later in life through some type of sickness or injury.[4]

Mark's use of *mogilalos* shows a clear allusion to the Greek version of Isaiah 35:6: "Then will the lame leap like a deer, and the mute tongue [*mogilalos*] shout for joy."[5] Mark sees in this miracle another fulfillment of Old Testament prophecy in Jesus's ministry. In the healing of the paralytic, Jesus caused the lame man to walk; here He looses the mute tongue.

Jesus pulled the man aside from the crowd. This was likely done for several reasons. First of all, Jesus wanted to avoid the praise and acclaim of the crowd.[6] Another reason that Jesus pulled the man aside from the crowd was to remove distractions. The deaf man probably had no idea what was going on and Jesus wanted to be able to minister to him without everyone crowding around them. The third reason that Jesus sought some measure of privacy was so that He could establish personal contact with the man.[7] This man probably had no knowledge of Jesus. Jesus wanted to let the man know that He cared about Him and understood his illness. While not explicitly mentioned, Jesus's compas-

---

2. Lane, *Mark*, 266.
3. Brooks, *Mark*, 122–23.
4. Lane, ibid.
5. John, *The Meaning*, 120.
6. Brooks, *Mark*, 123.
7. Lane, ibid.

sion is clearly demonstrated in this story. Because of the man's deafness, touch was the primary way that Jesus could show His concern.

After taking the deaf man aside, Jesus put His fingers in his ears. Jesus then spit and touched the saliva to the man's tongue and looked up to heaven. These three actions by Jesus mimed the man's "need, the process of healing, and the source from which such healing alone could come, in a way in which even a deaf mute could understand."[8] In this way, Jesus established some measure of faith in the man. As in the case of the paralytic, the vicarious faith of the friends got the person to Jesus. Now, however, the individual's faith must be engaged if he was going to receive something from God.

It should be noted, that while this use of saliva by Jesus might turn the stomach of a modern reader, this was a common practice in ancient days. Both Jewish and Hellenic sources acknowledged the healing powers present in the saliva of a holy man.[9] Mark 8:22–26 will provide another account of Jesus using saliva in the healing process. The Gospel of John also gives a dramatic account of the use of saliva in someone's healing.[10]

After touching the man in the areas of his infirmity, Jesus looked to heaven and sighed deeply. This indicates the strong emotion that Jesus felt. Human suffering evoked deep emotional responses from Jesus.[11] Mark highlights the range of Jesus's emotions more than any of the other Gospel writers. In looking to heaven here, Jesus was likely praying for God's help.[12]

At Jesus's command, "Be opened!" the man was healed. His "ears were opened, his tongue was loosened and he began to speak plainly." Mark provides us with the Aramaic phrase that Jesus used, "*Ephphatha!*" This phrase, and other Aramaic phrases that Mark includes, have lead some scholars to believe that Mark was having Jesus use these phrases as magical incantations in the pattern of other healers and wonder

---

8. Cole, *Mark*, 191.
9. Lane, *Mark*, 267.
10. John 9:6–7.
11. See Mark 1:41; Mark 3:5; John 11:33.
12. Brooks, *Mark*, 123.

workers.[13] What is much more likely is that Mark just wanted to include the exact phrase that Jesus used at the moment of healing.

This healing attracted a lot of attention, as would be expected. The man was speaking clearly now without any impediment and his ears were opened so that he could hear. As on other occasions, however, Jesus instructed the healed man and those who had seen the miracle to not tell anyone about it. However, also like on other occasions, the more Jesus told them not to talk about it, "the more they kept talking about it." Mark says that the crowd was "overwhelmed with amazement." Jesus was trying to keep the people quiet about the miracle to prevent a recurrence of what happened after He healed the leper. After that healing, Jesus was unable to even enter a town because of His fame.

It is ironic that, after giving a man his voice back, Jesus would order him to be quiet about it. While it was evidently frustrating for Jesus to have to deal with the publicity that miracles like this generated, it is hard to fault those who were involved. They were thoroughly amazed and said about Jesus, "He has done everything well. He even makes the deaf here and the mute speak." The language here reminds us of the creation story, in which after He had made everything, God "saw that it was good." Fuller notes, "The healing of the deaf mute is, after all, a Messianic act, a fulfillment of Old Testament prophecy and the restoration of the goodness of the original creation."[14] Mark again points the reader to the Divine power at work in Jesus. Not only were God's creative works perfect, so are the works of the Son.[15]

---

13. John, *The Meaning*, 120.
14. Fuller, *Interpreting*, 60–61.
15. Cole, *Mark*, 192.

19

The Feeding of the 4,000

During those days another large crowd gathered. Since they had nothing to eat, Jesus called his disciples to him and said, "I have compassion for these people; they have already been with me three days and have nothing to eat. If I send them home hungry, they will collapse on the way, because some of them have come a long distance." His disciples answered, "But where in this remote place can anyone get enough bread to feed them?" "How many loaves do you have?" Jesus asked. "Seven," they replied. He told the crowd to sit down on the ground. When he had taken the seven loaves, and given thanks, he broke them and gave them to his disciples to set before the people, and they did so. They had a few small fish as well; he gave thanks for them also and told the disciples to distribute them. The people ate and were satisfied. Afterward the disciples picked up seven basketfuls of broken pieces that were leftover. About four thousand men were present.

(MARK 8:1–9)

THIS SECOND miraculous feeding has been seen by many scholars as merely a retelling of the feeding of the 5000 from Mark 6:30–ff.[1] While the feeding of the 5000 is recorded in all four Gospels, Matthew is the only other evangelist besides Mark to record the feeding of the 4000. While Matthew provides some extra material about the type of ministry Jesus was doing during this three days of ministry, his account of the actual feeding miracle is almost identical to Mark's.[2]

---

1. Brooks, *Mark*, 124–25.
2. Matthew 15:29–39.

The Feeding of the 4,000

Mark clearly differentiates between the two feedings. There are several reasons why we should understand that Mark presented two separate miraculous feedings. First of all, the setting is very different. In the earlier feeding, Mark refers to the crowd being seated "on the green grass." Here, there is no mention of grass and from the disciples' comment about them being in a "remote place," one gets the feeling that they are in even more of an isolated location than before. There is also Jesus's reference to how far the people have traveled to be with Him. In discussing the location of this second feeding miracle, it should be noted also that this one appears to take place in a predominantly Gentile area.[3] It took place, "During those days," in which Jesus was ministering in areas that were mostly non-Jewish. So while the first feeding miracle took place in Jewish territory, here Jesus works a similar miracle in an area dominated by Gentiles.

Not only is the location of the two feedings different, the situation is different as well. In the first feeding, the crowd followed Jesus and His disciples as they were trying to find a place to be alone. Jesus spent the rest of the day teaching the crowd and performed the miraculous feeding late in the day. In the feeding of the 4000, this crowd had been with Jesus for three days. While Mark does not give us any details of that ministry time, Matthew tells us,

> Great crowds came to him, bringing the lame, the blind, the crippled, the dumb and many others, and laid them at his feet; and he healed them. The people were amazed when they saw the dumb speaking, the crippled made well, the lame walking and the blind seeing.[4]

While the first feeding miracle occurred after a day of teaching, the second feeding miracle occurred after three days of spectacular healings and miracles.

A third indicator that the feeding of the 4000 was separate from the feeding of the 5000 was the fact that Jesus referred to both miracles in a conversation He had with His disciples. In Mark 8:19–21, He reminds them of both miracles and asks them how much food was leftover from those two miraculous feedings. Jesus used both miracles to remind His disciples that He could provide for them, as well as to

3. Juel, *Mark*, 111.
4. Matthew 15:30–31.

trigger their faith in Who He was. After reminding the disciples of the two miracles, Jesus asked them, "Do you still not understand?"[5]

Another of the differences between the two feeding miracles is the fact that in the feeding of the 5000, the disciples took the initiative, asking Jesus to send the people away. In this story, Jesus takes the initiative and makes a statement of the problem to the disciples.[6] There response indicates that they are not expecting Jesus to repeat the miracle He performed with the crowd of 5000: "But where in this remote place can anyone get enough bread to feed them?"

In both feeding miracles, Jesus involved His disciples. They were not cognizant of His intention in either situation, yet He still made sure that they were part of the solution. In both miracles, Jesus blessed the food and then gave it to the disciples, who in turn, distributed to the multitude. After both miracles, the disciples gathered the leftovers. In this case there were seven basketfuls of leftovers.

This miracle again provides the reader with the assurance that Jesus is able to meet all of our needs. The many broken pieces that were left over "are the symbol of the inexhaustible spiritual food which is not diminished by being used."[7] If the two miraculous feedings are allusions to the Last Supper, Jesus is seen as the Bread that was broken for us and nourishes us our deepest spiritual hunger.

At the same time, we must never lose sight of the fact that this miracle, like so many that Jesus performed, was performed in response to human need. The primary purpose of this feeding "is to meet the physical needs of the multitude, who chose to be nourished by Jesus's word rather than bread."[8] The primary motive of Jesus's ministry was to minister to and serve those in need. As Jesus said, "I have compassion for these people . . ." That compassion was the driving force behind Jesus doing the things that He did.

---

5. Mark 8:21.
6. Juel, *Mark*, 111.
7. Richardson, *Miracle Stories*, 95.
8. Lane, *Mark*, 273.

20

The Two Touch Healing

They came to Bethsaida, and some people brought a blind man and begged Jesus to touch him. He took the blind man by the hand and led him outside the village. When he had spit on the man's eyes and put his hands on him, Jesus asked, "Do you see anything?" He looked up and said, "I see people; they look like trees walking around." Once more Jesus put his hands on the man's eyes. Then his eyes were opened, his sight was restored, and he saw everything clearly. Jesus sent him home, saying, "Don't go into the village."

(MARK 8:22-26)

THIS MIRACLE and the healing of the deaf mute in 7:32-37 are closely related. The language is very similar and the way that Jesus performs the healings are also similar. Both appear to be alluding to Isaiah 35:5-6. Both miracle stories start with people bringing someone to Jesus who is in need of a healing. In both cases, however, they do not ask Jesus to heal the person. They only ask Him to touch them. In both accounts, Jesus takes the needy person aside, away from the crowd. Both stories also have Jesus using saliva to facilitate the healing.

Mark is the only one of the four Gospel writers to include this story in his Gospel. One of the reasons for this could be because of the apparent ineffectiveness of Jesus's power in this situation. The other writers might not want to have included a story that showed Jesus appearing to struggle to work a miracle. "An incomplete cure and a two-stage healing may have been thought by some to be discrediting to Jesus. This consideration may be why Matthew and Luke omitted the story."[1] This is the only healing account in any of the Gospels that require two applications of Jesus's power. There are, however, other instances in which Jesus was limited in what He was able to do. In Mark 6:5–6 it says, "He could not do any miracles there, except lay his hands on a few sick people and heal them. And he was amazed at their lack of faith." This could be a similar situation involving a lack of faith.[2] After Jesus had laid His hands on the blind man, He asked him, "Do you see anything?" Jesus seems to have perceived some lack of faith or He would not have asked this question. In other similar situations, Jesus had not had to ask any such question because the person was completely healed after one touch.

As with the healing of the deaf mute, Jesus led the blind man aside, outside the village. In doing so, He was establishing a personal relationship of trust with the man.[3] Since he was unable to see he had to trust whoever was leading him by the hand. Crowds followed Jesus everywhere He went. By taking the man outside the village, away from the crowd, Jesus was able to remove him from the distracting noise that might have hindered his healing.

It was after applying saliva to the man's eyes that Jesus asked him if he saw anything. As we mentioned in the discussion on the healing of the deaf mute in Chapter Eighteen, the ancient world believed that saliva had magical powers. Roman historians describe Vespasian's use of saliva to heal a blind man. The blind man told Vespasian that the god Sarapis had directed him in a dream to have Vespasian apply spit to his cheeks and eyes which apparently healed him.[4]

In response to Jesus's question of whether or not he could see anything, the man said, "I see people; they look like trees walking around." This is an interesting response from a man who was blind. If he had been born blind, he would have no concept of what trees looked like or any standards to judge objects by. The man must have

---

1. Brooks, *Mark*, 133.
2. Cole, *Mark*, 201.
3. Lane, *Mark*, 285.
4. Eve, "Spit in Your Eye," 3. Eve's article builds the case that Mark was familiar with this story and was responding to it in his account of Jesus using saliva. In fact, Eve says that "Mark deliberately shaped the Blind Man of Bethsaida with the Blind Man of Alexandria in mind," 17.

lost his sight at some point through sickness or injury. At any rate, his vision is still unclear at this point and his healing is not complete.

Jesus then touched the man a second time and, "his eyes were opened, his sight was restored, and he saw everything clearly." The result of Jesus's second touch was another spectacular healing. The man is now able to see clearly. He does not care that it took Jesus two touches to affect his healing. For this man, it is enough that he can now see.

Jesus had led this man outside the village to heal him. After the healing, Jesus sent him home but told him, "Don't go into the village." As we have seen on several other occasions in Mark, spectacular healings have actually hindered or interrupted some of Jesus's ministry plans.[5] While Jesus performed many kinds of miracles and healings on numerous occasions, He never wanted to be known as just a healer. His ministry was much deeper than that. Jesus's command to go home also emphasizes the man's healing. He no longer needs someone to lead him by the hand.[6]

This healing story very clearly occupies "a special symbolic role in Mark's narrative."[7] It traces the progression of the disciples from a state of blindness and lack of understanding to a place of spiritual sight and perception. This is indicated by the placement of the miracle and what follows it. The next passage deals with Peter's confession of faith.

> Jesus and his disciples went on to the villages around Caesarea Philppi. On the way he asked them, "Who do the people say I am?" They replied, "Some say John the Baptist; others say Elijah; and still others, one of the prophets." "But what about you?" he asked. "Who do you say I am?" Peter answered, "You are the Christ." Jesus warned them not to tell anyone about him. (Mark 8:27–30).

Mark seems to be drawing a parallel between the two-stage healing of the blind man and the still developing faith of the disciples. Peter is the spokesman for the disciples and in his confession that Jesus is the Christ, he is announcing that they have come to a place of perception of Who Jesus is. "Peter's confession offers the first evidence

---

5. Lane, *Mark*, 286.
6. Gundry, *Survey*, 143.
7. Johnson, *The Writings*, 174.

that light has penetrated the darkness; he has a glimmer of insight."[8] Their understanding is still limited, however, and the disciples are like the blind man, who after Jesus's first touch could see, but not very clearly. It will not be until after the resurrection that the disciples will be able to see "everything clearly."[9] Jesus's followers still may have blurry spiritual vision, but it is not a permanent state. An encounter with the resurrected Jesus would provide the "second touch" to the disciples' spiritual eyes.

Jeffrey John sees Mark's Gospel as a two act drama.[10] In the first half, Jesus revealed Himself through His teaching and miracles. The disciples, however, were unable to understand what they were seeing and hearing. Hence, we have Mark's reference to the disciples' hardened hearts in 6:52, and Jesus's question in 8:21, "Do you still not understand?" Here in the middle of the Gospel, Peter confesses Jesus as the Christ. From here on out, Jesus will begin the second phase of the revelation to His followers, namely that the Christ must suffer and die.

---

8. Juel, *Mark*, 117, He continues, "But as we learn, Peter's "insight" is no more functional than the blind man's glimpse of walking trees. The words, we learn are correct—but Peter and the disciples are nevertheless still in the dark. The two stages necessary for complete healing of the blind man—for total clarity of vision—may well foreshadow what must occur with the disciples as well."

9. Johnson, "Mark VIII. 22–26," 370–83.

10. John, *The Meaning*, 130–31. See also Brooks, *Mark*, 132–33.

21

The Transfiguration

And he said to them, "I tell you the truth, some who are standing here will not taste death before they see the kingdom of God come with power." After six days Jesus took Peter, James and John with him and led them up a high mountain, where they were all alone. There he was transfigured before them. His clothes became dazzling white, whiter than anyone in the world could bleach them. And there appeared before them Elijah and Moses, who were talking with Jesus. Peter said to Jesus, "Rabbi, it is good for us to be here. Let us put up three shelters—one for you, one for Moses and one for Elijah." (He did not know what to say, they were so frightened.) Then a cloud appeared and enveloped them, and a voice came from the cloud: "This is my Son, whom I love. Listen to him!" Suddenly, when they looked around, they no longer saw anyone with them except Jesus. As they were coming down the mountain, Jesus gave them orders not to tell anyone what they had seen until the Son of Man had risen from the dead. They kept the matter to themselves, discussing what "rising from the dead" meant.

(MARK 9:1–10)

THE TRANSFIGURATION story provides "a preview of the full establishment of the kingdom of God at Jesus' return."[1] In the first chapter of Mark, Jesus had had a vision of an open heaven and had heard a heavenly Voice. This vision appears to have been for His eyes only. In the sixth chapter of Mark, Jesus's glory was manifested as He walked across the lake to His disciples in the boat. They, however, misidentified Him as a ghost. Their fear prevented them from obtaining

---

1. Brooks, *Mark*, 141.

MIRACLES IN MARK

the revelation that Jesus wanted them to have. In the transfiguration account, Jesus's heavenly glory is manifested explicitly to three of His followers. This event is clearly oriented to them.

The transfiguration is linked to the passage that comes before it. Immediately preceding this supernatural experience, Jesus makes an enigmatic statement, "I tell you the truth, some who are standing here will not taste death before they see the kingdom of God come with power." Scholars continue to puzzle over this verse. Was Jesus actually saying that He would return in the lifetime of His hearers? A key to understanding what Jesus meant is the verse Mark uses to connect Jesus's statement in Mark 9:1 with the rest of the passage: "After six days Jesus took Peter, James and John with him . . ." Mark ties the transfiguration account to Jesus's statement about the kingdom of God coming with power by using a specific chronological timeframe as a connector. The "six days" may also be an allusion to Exodus 24:15–18.[2] After Moses had been on Mount Sinai for six days, God called to him from the cloud on the seventh day. "Then Moses entered the cloud as he went on up the mountain."

All scholars do not make this connection between Mark 9:1 and the transfiguration story.[3] Some would understand that Jesus was referring to a later event such as the resurrection. Others see the outpouring of the Holy Spirit on the Day of Pentecost as when the kingdom of God would come with power. Mark, however, clearly saw the connection between Jesus's statement and the transfiguration experience. At the same time, the transfiguration is clearly a precursor to both the resurrection and the outpouring of the Holy Spirit after Jesus's ascension.

Jesus again selects Peter, James, and John to accompany him. These were the same three that He took with Him inside the house when He raised Jairus's young daughter from the dead. Jesus will later take these three with him when He goes into Gethsemane to pray.[4] The same three, along with Andrew, will also be the recipients of the Olivet Discourse on the end times.[5]

---

2. Juel, *Mark*, 127.
3. Cole, *Mark*, 209. See also Brooks, *Mark*, 139.
4. Mark 14:33.
5. Mark 13:3–ff.

The Transfiguration

Peter will later refer to this experience in his second letter[6], where he says,

> We did not follow cleverly invented stories when we told you about the power and coming of our Lord Jesus Christ, but we were eyewitnesses of his majesty. For he received honor and glory from God the Father when the voice came to him from the Majestic Glory, saying, "This is my beloved Son, whom I love; with him I am well pleased." We ourselves heard this voice that came from heaven when we were with him on the sacred mountain.[7]

This was obviously a very important experience for those who witnessed it. John also seems to allude to this experience when he says,

> The Word became flesh and made his dwelling among us. We have seen his glory, the glory of the One and Only, who came from the Father, full of grace and truth.[8]

After Jesus led the three disciples up on the mountain, Mark emphasizes that "they were all alone." In 6:31, Jesus told His disciples after their ministry trip, "Come with me by yourselves to a quiet place and get some rest." In 7:33, while dealing with the deaf mute, Jesus "took him aside" from the crowd. In 8:23, when interacting with the blind man at Bethsaida, Jesus "led him outside the village." Here, Jesus takes these three disciples aside, up on a mountain by themselves. The fact that they were all alone is emphasized to show that Jesus has created a setting without distractions for the revelation that is to follow.

"There he was transfigured before them." He was *metamorphoō*. Our word "metamorphosis" is derived from this Greek word and indicates "a radical change . . . a complete transformation."[9] Jesus's physical appearance had become familiar to the disciples. They had been with Him daily for almost three years. Here, they see His physical appearance changed before their eyes. Rather than describing any change in

---

6. See Spell, *Peter and Paul*, for my discussion on the authorship of 2 Peter.
7. 2 Peter 1:16–18.
8. John 1:14.
9. Brooks, *Mark*, 142.

His physical features, however, Mark only points out that "His clothes became dazzling white, whiter than anyone in the world could bleach them." Schmidt translates it as, "intensely brilliant white."[10]

The shining, glistening character of Jesus's clothes reflects the Old Testament concept of the glory of God.[11] "In the OT the glory of God is always conceived as shining brilliance or bright light."[12] For a brief moment, the veil is pulled back and the disciples are allowed to see Jesus in all of His heavenly glory. The *metamorphoō* that Jesus undergoes completely transforms His appearance, yet there is no description of His physical appearance other than His clothes. In Peter's recount of this experience in his second letter he mentions being an eyewitness and hearing the heavenly voice, but also avoids specifically describing what he saw on the mountain.

While Peter, James and John are processing what they are seeing, Elijah and Moses appear, "who were talking with Jesus." How did the disciples know who they were? We can assume that Elijah and Moses were not wearing name tags. Possibly, because of their heightened spiritual condition, they just "knew." Perhaps there were some introductions or conversations that Mark did not record.

The significance of the presence of Moses and Elijah is that they represent the Law and the Prophets. Their appearance confirms that the Law and the Prophets bear witness to Jesus.[13] He is the fulfillment of the Scriptures. Moses and Elijah had also both undergone some type of transformation during their lives. Moses had a put a veil over his face because it shown with reflected glory after being in the Presence of God. Elijah was transformed when he was caught up to heaven in a chariot of fire.

Peter, ever quick to speak, addresses Jesus as "Rabbi." This is not the title that we would expect him to use on such an occasion as this. "Rabbi" is certainly a respectful term but we would expect Peter to use "Lord" after seeing Jesus's glory revealed. This may indicate that Peter used the title "Rabbi" so habitually, that even after seeing Jesus transfigured it was still natural for him to call Him "Rabbi."

10. Schmidt, *The Gospel of Mark*, 99.
11. Lane, *Mark*, 318.
12. Ibid.
13. Brooks, *Mark*, 142.

The Transfiguration

Peter asks Jesus if He would like them to build three tents, one for Jesus, one for Moses, and one for Elijah. Mark then tells the reader parenthetically that Peter "did not know what to say, they were so frightened." While we can excuse Peter's rambling because of his fear, his statements still show us a continued lack of understanding of Jesus's true nature, even after the transfiguration. In wanting to build tabernacles and stay on the mountain, Peter still had not grasped what Jesus's mission was. While His heavenly glory might have been manifested on the mountain, Jesus's transfiguration was "the prelude to the passion."[14] The road back to His glory would go through the Cross. Peter's suggestion of building three tabernacles also puts Moses and Elijah on the same level with Jesus.[15]

The desire to build three tents on the side of the mountain shows that Peter still has not quite understood that God has already made His dwelling among men in the person of Jesus. He is "the new Tabernacle of divine glory."[16] One of the unfortunate aspects of human nature is that we tend to want to institutionalize our experiences rather than let those experiences change us.

The group on the mountain was then enveloped by a cloud and a voice came from the cloud, "This is my Son, whom I love. Listen to him." The cloud is symbolic of God's presence, reminding us again of Moses on Mount Sinai. When Moses set the tabernacle up in the wilderness, "the cloud covered the Tent of Meeting, and the glory of the Lord filled the tabernacle. Moses could not enter the tent of meeting because the cloud had settled upon it, and the glory of the Lord filled the tabernacle."[17] God's Presence was also manifested in a cloud of glory when Solomon dedicated his temple in 2 Samuel 8:10–12.

The heavenly voice seems to be aimed at the disciples. At His baptism, the voice had said, "You are my Son, whom I love; with you I am well pleased." Here the voice says, "This is my Son, whom I love." The voice then adds, "Listen to him." This is the clearest revelation yet to the disciples of Who Jesus is. They have witnessed Jesus changed before their eyes, radiating His preincarnate glory. They have seen

---

14. Lane, *Mark*, 319.
15. Brooks, *Mark*, 142–43.
16. Lane, *Mark*, 321.
17. Exodus 40:34–35.

MIRACLES IN MARK

Moses and Elijah talking with Jesus. They have heard the voice of God speak from a cloud of glory affirming Jesus as His Son.

Then, just as suddenly as it started, it is over. Jesus looks "normal" again. He is wearing the same clothes He was wearing earlier and His appearance is that of any other Jewish man in the First Century. Moses and Elijah are gone. The cloud has vanished. The disciples are alone on the mountain with Jesus.

As they were coming down off the mountain, Jesus told the three disciples not to discuss what they had seen until after He had risen from the dead. The full meaning of this vision would only become clear after the resurrection.[18] In truth, many of Jesus's sayings and teaching would only become clear after He had been raised. For the disciples, the crucifixion and resurrection of Jesus would provide the last pieces of the puzzle. Jesus's teaching, interpreted post-resurrection, would finally make sense. This supernatural experience that the disciples shared with Jesus on a mountain would also become clear later on. As we saw earlier, Peter and John would interpret and write about their experiences many years later.[19]

---

18. Cole, *Mark*, 212.

19. James, the brother of John, was the first of the Twelve to be martyred (Acts 12:2) so we never get a chance to get his version of the transfiguration.

22

A Demon Possessed Boy

When they came to the other disciples, they saw a large crowd around them and the teachers of the law arguing with them. As soon as all the people saw Jesus, they were overwhelmed with wonder and ran to greet him. "What are you arguing with them about?" he asked. A man in the crowd answered, "Teacher, I brought you my son, who is possessed by a spirit that has robbed him of speech. Whenever it seizes him, it throws him to the ground. He foams at the mouth, gnashes his teeth and becomes rigid. I asked your disciples to drive out the spirit, but they could not." "O unbelieving generation," Jesus replied, "how long shall I stay with you? How long shall I put up with you? Bring the boy to me." So they brought him. When the spirit saw Jesus, it immediately threw the boy into a convulsion. He fell to the ground and rolled around, foaming at the mouth. Jesus asked the boy's father, "How long has he been like this?" "From childhood," he answered. "It has often thrown him into fire or water to kill him. But if you can do anything, take pity on us and help us." "If you can?" said Jesus. "Everything is possible for him who believes." Immediately the boy's father exclaimed, "I do believe; help me overcome my unbelief!" When Jesus saw that a crowd was running to the scene, he rebuked the evil spirit. "You deaf and mute spirit," he said, "I command you, come out of him and never enter him again." The spirit shrieked, convulsed him violently and came out. The boy looked so much like a corpse that many said, "He's dead." But Jesus took him by the hand and lifted him to his feet, and he stood up. After Jesus had gone indoors, his disciples asked him privately, "Why couldn't we drive it out?" He replied, "This kind can come out only by prayer."

(MARK 9:14–29)

MIRACLES IN MARK

After having just left the mountain of transfiguration, Jesus and His three disciples rejoined the rest of the Twelve in the midst of a crisis. It is not just any type of crisis but a situation of demon possession that the Nine were not able to exorcise. Some scholars have seen the crowd's being "overwhelmed with wonder" at the sight of Jesus to the Israelite's reaction to Moses when he returned from Mount Sinai after giving him up for dead.[1] "Both Moses and Jesus return to find people behaving as if they have no faith in God, and both react with indignant fury."[2] Others have seen a parallel in this encounter of Jesus with the power of Satan right after the transfiguration and the account of Jesus's temptation in the wilderness right after the vision and heavenly voice that He experienced after His baptism.[3]

Jesus observed some of the teachers of the law arguing with His disciples and a crowd around them. Jesus asked what they were arguing about. It is unclear which of the two groups He is addressing. Neither the disciples nor the teachers of the law answer His question. We can only speculate as to what they may have been arguing about. Perhaps the teachers of the law and the disciples were arguing about the best way to deal with this type of demonic possession. Perhaps the teachers of the law were challenging the disciples' authority to even attempt an exorcism.[4] Perhaps the teachers of the law were berating the disciples for their inability to heal the boy.[5]

A man in the crowd answered Jesus's question and told him about his son who was possessed by a spirit that was constantly trying to kill him. He then says, "I asked your disciples to drive out the spirit, but they could not." In Mark 6:13, we were told that the disciples "drove out many demons and anointed many sick people with oil and healed them." Jesus had given them authority to drive out evil spirits. The disciples were evidently successful in that particular ministry trip that Jesus had sent them on, yet here they were unable to set this boy

1. Juel, *Mark*, 131. See also Hurtado, *Mark*, 147.
2. John, *The Meaning*, 145.
3. Lane, *Mark*, 329.
4. Ibid., 330.
5. Brooks, *Mark*, 147. See also Cole, *Mark*, 214, "One wonders why these same scribes, instead of embarrassing the crestfallen disciples before the crowd, did not set about exorcising the demon themselves, as a proof of their orthodoxy."

A Demon Possessed Boy

free. Lane notes that "during Jesus' absence an attitude of unbelief and self-confidence, based on past success, had exposed them to failure."[6] When Jesus sent the disciples out on their successful mission trip, there is no indication that He was with them then either. They were operating independently in pairs. A lack of faith clearly plays a role in the disciples' failure because Jesus refers to them as an "unbelieving generation." We will find out later, however, that a lack of faith was only part of the reason that the disciples' could not cast the demon out of the boy.

Jesus then instructed that the boy be brought to him. At the moment that the spirits see Jesus, however, the demons began manifesting causing him to fall to the ground, convulse, roll around and foam at the mouth. Most commentators agree that this appears to be an epileptic seizure. Jeffrey John takes this a step further. He believes that this story originally involved Jesus healing an epileptic boy but that Mark changed it for his theological purposes, adding the demonic references.[7]

Along with the apparent epileptic symptoms, the boy is also deaf and mute. The symptoms of the boy are described in detail. While most scholars agree that the boy was showing all the symptoms of epilepsy, we still come back to the question of demon involvement that we have discussed in previous chapters. Jesus clearly attributed demonic influence to the boy's condition, going so far as to address it as a "deaf and mute spirit." As we have noted previously, Mark, along with other New Testament writers, draw clear distinctions between healings and exorcisms. This particular story, however, is not quite as black and white.

There are at least three possibilities here that are worth considering. First of all, the boy's condition was strictly demonic. In this case, the epileptic symptoms, deafness and muteness were all caused by the evil spirit. This does not mean that epilepsy is always synonymous with demon possession. It does mean that in this particular situation the demon possession produced symptoms that make it look like epilepsy. Another possibility is that this boy did have a medical condition that appeared to be epilepsy but that it was aggravated by a demonic presence that also rendered him deaf and mute. As Hendricksen puts it, "this was *not an ordinary* case of epilepsy but one brought about

6. Lane, *Mark*, 332.

7. John, *The Meaning*, 145–46. See also Fuller, *Interpreting*, 61–62.

and aggravated by a demon . . ."⁸ (his italics) If this is the case, we have a serious medical condition made even worse by the presence of demonic forces. The third possibility here is that this was completely a medical condition. It did not involve any demonic forces, and Jesus merely healed the lad like He had healed so many other people during His ministry.

The most likely answer is the second possibility discussed above. The boy did have a medical condition. It appeared to have been aggravated and intensified by demonic involvement. The chronic nervous disorder was made worse by the evil spirit. It is clear that the goal of the demon is the utter destruction of the boy. The father testified that the evil spirit had constantly thrown the boy to the ground, thrown him into fire and into the water in an effort to kill him.

After detailing his son's condition to Jesus, the father then says, "But if you can do anything, take pity on us and help us." Jesus quick reply focuses on the man's statement, "if you can." Jesus goes on to say, "Everything is possible for him who believes." The inability of the disciples' to help his son has apparently shaken the man's faith. Jesus, however, puts some responsibility back onto the father. Lane paraphrases verse 23, "As regards your remark about my ability to help your son, I tell you everything depends on your ability to believe, not on mine to act."⁹ Throughout his Gospel, Mark has demonstrated that faith is the attitude that moves God. It is not always perfect faith, or even complete faith, yet people who have reached out to Jesus with whatever faith they have been the recipients of His power. The writer to the Hebrews reminds us "And without faith it is impossible to please God, because anyone who comes to him must believe that he exists and that he rewards those who earnestly seek him."[10]

The father's reply comes from the depths of his heart, "I do believe; help me overcome my unbelief!" He is declaring that he is a part of the "unbelieving generation" that Jesus had just mentioned. At the same time, he is reaching out to Jesus with what faith that he does have. The very fact that he had brought his son to Jesus in the first place indicates a level of belief. In a very real sense, this statement describes all of us. We

---

8. Hendricksen, *Mark*, 348.
9. Lane, *Mark*, 333.
10. Hebrews 11:6.

all start at a place of unbelief and move towards a place of faith. As our relationship with God grows, so does our faith in Him.

As Jesus saw the crowd growing, He rebuked the spirit and said, "You deaf and mute spirit, I command you, come out of him and never enter him again." This produced quite a reaction. "The spirit shrieked, convulsed him violently and came out." Even at the moment of exorcism, the spirit appeared intent on harming the boy. The spirit left so violently that many in the crowd that the boy was dead. Jesus took him by the hand and lifted him up.

While it is unclear whether or not the boy actually died here and was raised up by Jesus, it is clear that Mark parallels this account with the raising of Jairus's daughter.[11] The verb that Mark uses for "he stood up," is *anistēmi*. This is the same word used when Jesus raised Jairus's daughter from the dead. It is also used in Acts 9:41 where Peter raises Tabitha from the dead and in 1 Thessalonians 4:16 where Paul says, "the dead in Christ shall rise . . ." At the very least, Mark is telling us that Jesus gave this young man his life back by delivering him from Satan's power.

When the disciples were alone with Jesus again, they asked him why they had not been able to cast the spirit out. Jesus answer was, "This kind can only come out by prayer." A lack of faith ("unbelieving generation") and a lack of prayer tend to go together. Prayer strengthens our faith, which in turn helps us to see how much we need to pray.

Jesus statement to His disciples about prayer implies that all demons are not equal. Some are stronger than others and require more than a simple command to make them leave. Could it be that the disciples attempted to cast the demon out of the boy and then gave up when nothing had happened? Is it possible that if they had persevered, gone to prayer, and stay focused on seeing the boy delivered that they could have seen him set free? I think that this is the case. Just because the disciples had been successful before in casting out demons is no guarantee that they would be successful in the future. "Rather the power of God must be asked for on each occasion in radical reliance upon his ability alone."[12] One important aspect of faith is that of perseverance. If the disciples had not given up, I believe that they could have seen the boy set free.

11. Brooks, *Mark*, 148.
12. Lane, *Mark*, 335–36.

MIRACLES IN MARK

I will close this chapter on a personal note. On a mission trip to India in 2000, we were holding an outdoor crusade at a Hindu village. After the service, a young woman of about twenty five years came forward for prayer. As soon as we started praying for her, it became very clear that she had some demonic issues. They started physically manifesting through her by writhing, moaning, and covering her ears to block out the music and our prayers. This turned out to be one of those situations in which the demons really did not want to leave. She physically attacked one of the Indian pastors and kept yelling at us. The demons were very abusive in their taunts. Several of us prayed for this girl for two hours before we finally were able to expel the demons from her. We led her in a prayer of commitment to Christ and left her with several of the women from the local church.

By this time it was late and we were all exhausted and just wanted to go back to the hotel and go to bed. The local pastor, however, had arranged a meal for us at his church. When we got there a little later, we noticed that one of the women who was serving us was the one we had spent two hours praying for. She was radiant as she thanked us over and over for what we had done for her. This was definitely one of those situations that Jesus had described in which the demons would only come out by faith filled, persistent prayer.

23

The Healing of Bartimaeus

Then they came to Jericho. As Jesus and his disciples, together with a large crowd, were leaving the city, a blind man, Bartimaeus (that is, the Son of Timaeus), was sitting by the roadside begging. When he heard that it was Jesus of Nazareth, he began to shout, "Jesus, Son of David, have mercy on me!" Many rebuked him and told him to be quiet, but he shouted all the more, "Son of David, have mercy on me!" Jesus stopped and said, "Call him." So they called to the blind man, "Cheer up! On your feet! He's calling you." Throwing his cloak aside, he jumped to his feet and came to Jesus. "What do you want me to do for you?" Jesus asked him. The blind man said, "Rabbi, I want to see." "Go," said Jesus, "your faith has healed you." Immediately he received his sight and followed Jesus along the road.

(MARK 10:46–52)

THIS IS the last healing miracle recorded in Mark. Earl Johnson says that "it is hardly accidental that the final healing miracle in the gospel involves the giving of sight to a blind man and occurs at the last possible moment before the passion."[1] Mark has alluded to the spiritual blindness and deafness of the disciples in several locations throughout his Gospel. At the same time, he has presented several healing miracles in which Jesus heals those who are blind and deaf. Mark shows that Jesus not only wants to heal physical blindness and deafness He wants to heal spiritual blindness and deafness as well.

As with so many of Jesus's miracles, this one takes place in the context of a crowd. By this point in His ministry, Jesus's popularity was such that He could not go anywhere without attracting a large following. Many scholars see this healing as the concluding miracle in this section of Mark. The section opened with the healing of the blind

---

1. Johnson., "Mark 10:46–52," 198.

man at Bethsaida in 8:22–26. This arrangement of these stories has the two healings acting "like bookends to hold this material together."[2]

The vividness of this story has all the elements of an eyewitness account. Perhaps this is another story that Mark is quoting verbatim from Peter. The presence of a blind beggar, sitting on the side of the road was and is a common sight in many parts of the world. It is significant that Bartimaeus's name is preserved. Mark is the only one of the Gospel writers to name the beggar. The Gospel writers rarely provided the names of those who were healed. The inclusion of Bartimaeus's name may indicate that he later became known in the Church.[3]

As a blind man, Bartimaeus had to rely on his other senses. He heard the crowd moving by him. He could feel the "buzz" in the air. The beggar evidently had some knowledge of Jesus, because as soon as he heard that it was Jesus who was passing by, Bartimaeus began shouting out, "Jesus, Son of David, have mercy on me!" It is interesting to note that, "Many rebuked him and told him to be quiet." Usually the crowds were eager to see Jesus perform miracles. Here the crowd appears to try and prevent Bartimaeus from getting to Jesus.

Instead of being quiet, however, Bartimaeus "shouted all the more, '"Son of David, have mercy on me."'" This reference to Jesus as the "Son of David" is clearly a messianic reference. This title is not just a reference to Jesus as a descendant of David, but understands that He is the One "who is to inherit and fulfill the promises made to David" in the Old Testament.[4] Up to this point in Mark, other than Peter's confession of Jesus as the Messiah, no one else has recognized this truth (not counting the demonic confessions, of course!). The irony is clear. This blind man sees the truth that is hidden from others.[5]

Bartimaeus's persistent shouts got Jesus's attention. Jesus called for the beggar to be brought to Him. The same people, who had just been telling Bartimaeus to be quiet, now tell him, "Cheer up! On your feet! He's calling you!" In Mark's Gospel, Jesus is shown as always having time for those who call on Him in faith to help them. Bartimaeus already had a measure of faith or he would not have cried out for Jesus

2. Hurtado, *Mark*, 173.
3. Lane, *Mark*, 387.
4. Brooks, *Mark*, 173
5. Juel, *Mark*, 149.

The Healing of Bartimaeus

in the first place. Jesus's call to him would have served to create a sense of anticipation and hope in Bartimaeus. It would have strengthened his faith and prepared him for his encounter with Jesus.

Without hesitation, the beggar threw his cloak aside, jumped to his feet and came to Jesus. Mark does not spare us any detail. The cloak would have been spread out in front of him to receive alms.[6] Bartimaeus is already anticipating his healing in casting the garment aside. He will not be begging anymore. The cloak also symbolizes anything that would have held the beggar back. When worn, it was loose fitting and long and could have tripped him up.[7] He throws it aside so that nothing will slow him down as he rushes to get to Jesus.

When Bartimaeus managed to get to Jesus, the Lord asked him, "What do you want me to do for you?" While this may seem like an obvious question, Jesus wanted to hear it from the man himself. He had been asking for alms from the passersby. Did he want a handout or a healing? Jesus wanted Barimaeus to express what he wanted the most. Jesus often established a relationship with the person that He healed through His conversation with them. Bartimaeus told Jesus, "Rabbi, I want to see." This statement indicates his belief that Jesus can heal him.

Jesus questioning of Bartimaeus also provides an interesting contrast with the passage that comes right before this one. There, James and John, the sons of Zebedee, came to Jesus with a request. Jesus asked them the same question He asked Bartimaeus, "What do you want me to do for you?"[8] They asked Jesus that one of them be allowed to sit on Jesus's right and the other on His left when He established His kingdom. This request showed that they were still blind and did not understand the true nature of Jesus's kingdom. As He goes on to say, His kingdom is built on serving others. "For even the Son of Man did not come to be served, but to serve, and to give his life as a ransom for many."[9] Bartimaeus's request, on the other hand, was much more in keeping with what Jesus came to do: to save, heal, and restore people.

---

6. Lane, *Mark*, 388.
7. Hendriksen, *Mark*, 421.
8. Mark 10:36.
9. Mark 10:45.

This idea of Bartimaeus having to tell Jesus what he wanted is an important prayer principle for us to remember. God always knows what we want and what we need. However, it is important that we voice our needs and wants to God. The very act of asking expresses faith. If we are too busy or proud to bring our needs before God, we cannot expect anything. If, however, we come into the presence of God on a regular basis, with humble and thankful hearts, making our requests known to God, we are going to see our prayers answered.

Bartimaeus's faith in Jesus was vindicated. In a moment, he went from a world of darkness to a world of light and color. This time, there was no special touch from Jesus; no application of saliva. Jesus's word alone is enough. "Go, your faith has healed you." The word Mark uses for "healed" is a derivative of *sōzō* in the Greek.[10] Jesus uses the same phrase in Mark 5:34 where the woman with the bleeding condition was healed. It can be translated "saved" as well as "healed." Mark probably intended this double meaning. "The man was healed physically and saved spiritually."[11] His faith purchased more than just his healing. His faith brought him into a saving relationship with Jesus.

After telling the reader that Bartimaeus received his sight, Mark says that he "followed Jesus along the road." This is a picture of discipleship. Faith plus following Jesus indicate someone who has become a disciple. The very fact that his name is remembered indicates that Bartimaeus probably did become a follower of Jesus.[12] Before, the blind beggar had been sitting on the side of the road, hoping someone would throw him a few coins. After encountering Jesus, Bartimaeus has his sight and is following Him down the road with the rest of the excited crowd.

---

10. The root word is *sōzō*, which means, "to save, keep safe, preserve, protect, spare," Feyerabend, *Pocket Dictionary*, 371.

11. Brooks, *Mark*, 174. See also Luke 7:50.

12. Brooks, ibid.

24

Cursing a Fig Tree

The next day as they were leaving Bethany, Jesus was hungry. Seeing in the distance a fig tree in leaf, he went to find out if it had any fruit. When he reached it, he found nothing but leaves, because it was not the season for figs. Then he said to the tree, "May no one ever eat fruit from you again." And his disciples heard him say it. In the morning, as they went along, they saw the fig tree withered from the roots. Peter remembered and said to Jesus, "Rabbi, look! The fig tree you cursed has withered!" "Have faith in God," Jesus answered. "I tell you the truth, if anyone says to this mountain, 'Go, throw yourself into the sea, and does not doubt in his heart but believes that what he says will happen, it will be done for him. Therefore I tell you, whatever you ask for in prayer, believe that you have received it, and it will be yours. And when you stand praying, if you hold anything against anyone, forgive him, so that your father in heaven may forgive your sins.

(MARK 11:12–14; 20–25)

THIS STORY is by far the most difficult of the miracles to understand in Mark's Gospel. It is destructive in nature and in some ways resembles the miracle stories found in the apocryphal Infancy Gospels.[1] In reality, however, this story is full of rich symbolism and imagery. As Lane says, "Events have meaning beyond their face value; they become significant as they are interpreted."[2] It appears that Jesus imitated Old Testament prophets and acted out a prophetic parable when He cursed

---

1. Juel, *Mark*, 155. Juel goes on to say, "The picture of Jesus is unflattering, and the miracle is devoid of religious significance."

2. Lane, *Mark*, 400.

the fig tree. This is a staged event for His disciples' (and readers') benefit. Jesus is following the example of Isaiah, Jeremiah, Ezekiel, Hosea, and other Old Testament prophets by cursing the barren fig tree.

In Isaiah 20, God had the prophet walk around "stripped and barefoot for three years," to signal the judgment that would be coming on Egypt and Cush. In Ezekiel 4, God had the prophet to lay on his left side for 390 days and then on his right side for 40 days "bearing" the sins of Israel and Judah, respectively. Hosea's marriage to the prostitute, Gomer, was used by God to symbolize His relationship with His wayward people. Jesus's curse on the fig tree fits in with this prophetic tradition of occasionally acting parables out. The symbolic actions of the Old Testament prophets usually conveyed a message of judgment on the nation, whether it was Judah or Israel. The symbolic action of cursing the tree also provides a message of judgment on the nation, even though Jesus does not explicitly explain it.

It is important to note how Mark sets this passage up. In verses 12–14, Jesus observes the fig tree in leaf but does not find any fruit on it. By all outward appearances it should have fruit on it. After finding none, He speaks to the tree and says, "May no one ever eat fruit from you again." Immediately after this happens, Mark records in verse

> On reaching Jerusalem, Jesus entered the temple area and began driving out those who were buying and selling there. He overturned the tables of the money changers and the benches of those selling doves, and would not allow anyone to carry merchandise through the temple courts. And as he taught them, he said, "Is it not written: "'My house will be called a house of prayer for all nations'? But you have made it 'a den of robbers.'"
>
> The chief priests and the teachers of the law heard this and began looking for a way to kill him, for they feared him, because the whole crowd was amazed at his teaching. When evening came, they went out of the city.

It is the next morning after this cleansing of the temple that Mark records that the disciples saw the fig tree that Jesus had cursed, now withered from the roots up. Peter remembered what Jesus had said and pointed it out to Him, "Rabbi, look! The fig tree you cursed has withered!"

The placement of the account of Jesus's cleansing of the temple between the account of the curse of the fig tree and Peter's discovery that it had withered from the roots up, indicate that Jesus is linking the tree to the Jewish nation. The cursing of the fig tree will serve to interpret Jesus's visit to the temple.[3] The fig tree was often used as a symbol of the nation of Israel.[4] Here, Jesus seems to draw a parallel between the fig tree, whose outward appearance indicates fruit, with the temple, whose beauty and magnificent ceremonies also indicate fruit. In reality, however, both are barren and devoid of fruit. Jesus came to the temple looking for spiritual fruit but did not find any.[5] It is not surprising that in 13:1-2 Jesus pronounces judgment on the temple, saying, "Not one stone will be left on another; everyone will be thrown down." This language is reminiscent of His cursing of the fig tree. Just as Jesus expelled the merchants from the temple, so were the religious leaders that authorized the merchants about to be expelled from their seat of authority.[6]

Jesus's judgment on Israel and their religious institutions seems to be based on a couple of factors. First of all, the religious establishment had chosen the ritual practices of the Law instead of a relationship with God. This is what they were teaching the masses. In 7:1-23, Jesus addresses this issue in depth. He quotes Isaiah 29:13,

> *These people honor me with their lips, but their hearts are far from me. They worship me in vain; their teachings are but rules taught by men.*

Jesus tells the religious leaders that they had "let go of the commands of God and are holding on to the traditions of men."

Jesus goes on in this passage to discuss the importance of keeping our hearts pure. He tells the crowd that it is only what comes out of their hearts that make them unclean. The religious leaders placed a great significance on maintaining ritual purity by doing certain rituals (ceremonial washing, maintaining a strict kosher diet, avoiding certain groups of people, etc) yet their hearts were filled with hatred towards Jesus and the "sinners" that He reached out to.

In 12:28-34, Jesus is asked by one of the teachers of the law, probably a scribe, which one of the commandments was the greatest.

3. Juel, *Mark*, 156.
4. See Jeremiah 29:17; Hosea 9:10, 16; Joel 1:7; Micah 7:1.
5. Cole, *Mark*, 250.
6. Brooks, *Mark*, 180.

MIRACLES IN MARK

This is possibly a sincere question from one who was a genuine seeker of God. It could also have been that this scribe was looking for a basis in which he could accuse Jesus. Either way, Jesus seemed to earn his respect by His answer. Jesus summarized the entire Law in two commands. The first was to, "Love the Lord your God with all your heart and with all your soul and with all your mind and with all your strength." The second was to, "Love your neighbor as yourself." Jesus cut through all the religious ceremony and ritual to what was essential. The scribe who had asked the question even acknowledged that Jesus had answered well. In mass, however, the religious leaders had moved beyond the simplicity of loving God and loving people and created an institution based on rules that allowed them to maintain power over the people.

Another reason for Jesus's judgment is the fact that while the merchants were busy changing money and selling sacrificial animals in the temple courtyard, the religious leaders were inside the temple plotting to take Jesus's life. He was the One whose life provided meaning for the sacrifices that were being offered, yet the religious establishment did not recognize it. This would culminate in the crucifixion of Jesus by the Romans at the instigation of the Jews. In their rejection of Jesus, the Jews would lose their preeminence in the purpose of God.

While this interpretation of the cursing of the fig tree has been the accepted one throughout Church history, it really did not come from Jesus's own lips.[7] He does not interpret His prophetic parable. He leaves it to others to interpret. Instead, when Peter points out that the fig tree had withered, Jesus launched into a discourse on faith, prayer, and forgiveness.

Throughout His ministry, Jesus stressed the importance of faith. After calming the storm, Jesus asked His disciples, "Why are you so afraid? Do you still have no faith?"[8] He told both the woman with the issue of blood and Bartimaeus, after they were healed, "your faith has healed you."[9] After being told that his daughter was dead, Jesus told Jairus, "Don't be afraid; just believe."[10] When He visited His home-

---

7. Oden and Hall, *Ancient Christian Commentary*, 158–59.
8. Mark 4:40.
9. Mark 5:34 and 10:52.
10. Mark 5:36.

Cursing a Fig Tree

town of Nazareth, He could not do many miracles there. "And he was amazed at their lack of faith."[11] When confronted by the demon possessed boy that the disciples could not cure, Jesus told the boy's father, "Everything is possible for him who believes."[12]

Jesus now uses the withered fig tree as an object lesson of what is possible for someone who has faith. He goes on to tell them that if they do not doubt in their heart, they could cast the Mount of Olives into the nearby Dead Sea.[13] Obviously, this is a figure of speech. The principle, however, is that there are mountains in our lives and the lives of those that we minister to that we can literally cast out of the way in prayer by faith. These mountains might take the form of sickness, unhealthy habits, poverty, or addictions. Jesus demonstrated over and over again that faith leads to miracles.

Jesus makes an incredible statement about prayer in verse 24: "Therefore, I tell you, whatever you ask for in prayer, believe that you have received it, and it will be yours." Faith is not described here as just an aspect of prayer. It should be the way that we relate to God. As the writer to the Hebrews put it, "And without faith it is impossible to please God, because anyone who comes to him must believe that he exists and that he rewards those who earnestly seek him."[14] Jesus is telling His followers to have confidence that when they pray, God is hearing them and working on their behalf. As a wise man said, "We will never see the impossible done until we connect with the invisible." God has shown His power throughout history to those with "the risky commitment of faith."[15]

It is appropriate that Jesus discusses prayer here after His cleansing of the temple. He quoted Isaiah 56:7, when He said, "Is it not written: "My house will be called a house of prayer for all nations?" Rather than seeing dead traditions and rituals acted out in the temple, Jesus longed to see people connecting with God through genuine prayer. The moneychangers had evidently set up in the Court of the Gentiles, thereby excluding them from the one area of the temple that was

---

11. Mark 6:6.
12. Mark 9:23.
13. See Chapter 25 for another alternative to the Mount of Olives.
14. Hebrews 11:6.
15. English, *The Message of Mark*, 189.

open to them. All people should have access to God, whether Jews or Gentiles.

Jesus's discussion of prayer also includes the important aspect of forgiveness. While faith is how we relate to God and is what shapes our prayers, forgiveness is the way that we relate to other people. It is only as we forgive others that we can expect to have our own sins forgiven. The context here also seems quite clear that we cannot expect to see our prayers answered if we have not forgiven someone who might have sinned against us.

25

God's Greatest Sign

And they crucified him. Dividing up his clothes, they cast lots to see what each would get ... With a loud cry, Jesus breathed his last. The curtain of the temple was torn in two from top to bottom. And when the centurion, who stood there in front of Jesus, heard his cry and saw how he died, he said, "Surely this man was the Son of God."

(MARK 15:24, 37–39)

IN CHAPTER one, we discussed the confrontation between Jesus and the Pharisees in Mark 8:11–12. The Pharisees came to Jesus and asked Him for a sign. Mark's Gospel is full of miracles and supernatural events. The Pharisees were eyewitnesses on several occasions in which Jesus worked miracles.[1] These miracles and healings were not the kinds of signs that the Pharisees were looking for, as we discussed. Jesus flatly refused to give them a sign.

Here, at the end of His ministry, however, Jesus provides a sign for all who have the eyes to see it in the crucifixion. To be sure, the religious leaders saw no significance or revelation in Jesus's death. In fact, His death had been their intention for the last couple of years. The irony is that this was Jesus's goal all along, as well. He had told His followers, "For even the Son of Man did not come to be served, but to serve, and to give his life as a ransom for many."[2] The cross was

---

1. See 2:1-ff; 8:1-ff; 9:14-ff provide three examples. There are several other situations that refer to large crowds being around as Jesus healed and this could imply the presence of religious leaders in the crowd.
2. Mark 10:45.

ultimately the fulfillment of the commission that Jesus had received from God at the time of His baptism.[3]

The actual event of the crucifixion is described by Mark with minimal detail.[4] Those who lived under Roman rule would have been all too familiar with the way that the practice was carried out. Mel Gibson's 2004 film, "The Passion of the Christ," probably visualizes and depicts the crucifixion in as realistic terms as any movie can. Needless to say, crucifixion, as a form of torture and execution, really did not have an equal in the ancient world. This practice did much to help the Romans to maintain control over their vast empire.

While He was hanging on the cross, Jesus not only had to endure the physical pain and anguish or the emotional pain of feeling abandoned by God, He also had to endure the mockery and taunts of the religious leaders and those who were passing by. Mark records,

> *Those who passed by hurled insults at him, shaking their heads and saying, "So! You who are going to destroy the temple and build it in three days, come down from the cross and save yourself." In the same way the chief priests and the teachers of the law mocked him among themselves. "He saved others," they said, "but he can't save himself! Let this Christ, this king of Israel, come down from the cross, that we may see and believe." Those crucified with him also heaped insults on him.*[5]

Paradoxically, there is much truth to these taunts. "If Jesus was to fulfill his mission on behalf of men he could not save himself from the sufferings appointed by God."[6] Jesus had taught His followers He would "be rejected by the elders, chief priests and teachers of the law, and that he must be killed and after three days rise again."[7] Ultimately, the salvation of mankind hinged on Jesus not saving Himself.

The taunt about Jesus destroying the temple and building it in three days deserves closer scrutiny. While Jesus makes a similar statement in John's Gospel in John 2:19, He does not make this claim in

3. Tannehill, "The Gospel of Mark," 88.
4. Lane, *Mark*, 564.
5. Mark 15:29–32.
6. Lane, *Mark*, 569–70. See also, Carroll and Green, *The Death of Jesus*, 28. "By refusing to save his own life, he saves others."
7. Mark 8:29–31.

Mark. In fact, Mark has someone else put the claim in Jesus's mouth at His trial: "We heard him say, 'I will destroy this manmade temple and in three days will build another, not made by man.'"[8] It is likely, however, that there is some basis for the accusation. In John, Jesus had responded to a request for a miraculous sign to prove His authority by saying, "Destroy this temple, and I will raise it again in three days." John interprets this statement for us by saying, "But the temple he had spoken of was his body."[9]

Mark leaves us to interpret the accusation in 14:58 and the taunt in 15:29-30 for ourselves. The passage in 11:11-ff provides us with some insight about Jesus's relationship with the temple. Before He entered the temple in Jerusalem, He cursed the fig tree for not bearing fruit. He then went into the temple and confronted those who were buying and selling there, overturned the moneychanger's tables, and would not let anyone carry merchandise through the temple courts. Achtemeier understands Jesus's actions as His "prophetic-symbolic act of ending cultic worship within the temple."[10] In the previous chapter we discussed Jesus's prophetic-symbolic act of cursing the fig tree. Here that same terminology is applied to Jesus's actions in the temple courts.

The next day, Peter pointed out to Jesus the withered fig tree, the very one that He had cursed the day before. Jesus then answered him by speaking about faith. Jesus's first statement, however, involved saying to "this mountain, 'Go, throw yourself into the sea.'" Which "mountain" was Jesus talking about here? Most commentators understand that Jesus is referring to the Mount of Olives. On the other hand, could Jesus be making a reference here to the overthrow of the temple and its institutions? Jesus's actions in the temple are usually referred to as His cleansing of the temple. Mark seems to also see that event as the cursing of the temple.[11] It is possible that Jesus was not referring to the Mount of Olives, but instead to the Temple Mount.[12] Perhaps He gestured to the Temple Mount when He made the statement about throwing itself into the sea, speaking figuratively about the overthrow

---

8. Mark 14:58.
9. John 2:21.
10. Achtemeier, *Mark*, 24.
11. Carroll and Green, *The Death of Jesus*, 32.
12. Ibid.

of the temple and its institutions. Obviously this is speculation, but if fits with the context of the prophetic parable that Jesus is acting out in Mark 11.[13]

Mark does not allow the reader to forget about the temple and Jesus's proclamation of its downfall. In 13:1-2, the disciples point out the beauty of its buildings: "Look, teacher! What massive stones! What magnificent buildings!" Jesus's answer was probably not what the disciples were expecting. "Do you see all these great buildings? Not one stone here will be left on another; everyone will be thrown down." With the destruction of Jerusalem in AD 70, about a million Jews killed, and the temple being sacked and burned, Palestinian Judaism was, for all practical purposes, dead.[14] This event was seen by the first century Church as the fulfillment of Jesus' prophecy.

Now as Jesus hangs on the cross, the subject of the temple comes up again. The religious leaders use His statement about destroying the temple and Jesus rebuilding it in three days as a taunt. They obviously do not understand the allegory that Jesus was using. In their minds, the idea of the temple being destroyed is clearly an impossibility forgetting the fact that it had been destroyed once before. Their decision to crucify Jesus, however, has sealed the fate of the temple and all that it represents. As Juel notes, "The execution of Jesus will have dire consequences for the temple, however unlikely that may now appear."[15]

Jesus was crucified at the third hour or about nine in the morning. At the sixth hour or around noon, darkness covered the land until the ninth hour or three in the afternoon. After hanging on the cross for six hours, Jesus gave a loud cry and "breathed his last." This reminds the hearer of the commissioning sequence in chapter one in which the Holy Spirit came onto (and by implication of the Greek *into*) Jesus. At his death, He seems to expel the Spirit.[16] At this moment, Mark notes that two things happened. The first was that at the moment of Jesus's death, "The curtain of the temple was torn in two, from top to bottom." The second thing that happened was that when the attending Roman

---

13. See chapter 11 for more on the use of the prophetic parable.
14. Cole, *Mark*, 273. See also, Hendriksen, *Mark*, 512-13.
15. Juel, *Mark*, 221.
16. Dowd and Malbon, "The Significance," 296. In John, Jesus breathes on His disciples in an impartation of the Spirit (John 20:22). The same idea seems to be expressed here by Mark at the moment of Jesus's death.

centurion, "who stood there in front of Jesus, heard his cry and saw how he died, he said, "Surely this man was the Son of God."

In describing the curtain being torn in two, Mark takes us back to the beginning of Jesus's ministry, when God gave Him the vision of the heavens being torn open at His baptism. The word that Mark uses to describe the curtain being torn is a derivative of *schizō*. The root word is the same as in 1:10 when Jesus had His vision of Heaven being torn open. At the beginning of Jesus's ministry, He had a vision of heaven being ripped open. Here at the moment of His death the veil or curtain in the temple that covered the Holy of Holies was ripped open. This was "the shielding curtain" described in Exodus 26:31-35 and 40:20-21. It was designed to keep people out. Only the priest was allowed to enter the Most Holy Place, and that was only once a year.

The concept here is stunning. As Jesus dies, God pulls the "veil" away from His face in the ultimate theophany.[17] God's "face" or "presence" had for years been hidden behind the veil in the Most Holy Place. Now, at the moment of Jesus's death God is showing His "face" in His Son. This is the ultimate picture of self-revelation. Access to the Divine Presence is now available for everyone. This includes the Gentile centurion who will be the first non-Jew to recognize Jesus's true identity.[18] Jesus's death did not mean an end to the presence of God on the Earth. On the contrary, with the tearing of the curtain in the Temple, God's presence was now being released to the whole world, Gentiles as well as the Jews.[19]

Mark had told us earlier in the chapter that when Jesus was crucified there was a sign, probably affixed to the cross, with the charge against Him: "The King of the Jews."[20] This idea of His kingship was also part of the taunts He had to endure while hanging on the cross. "Let this Christ, this King of Israel, come down now from the cross, that we may see and believe." Now, at the moment of His death, Mark shows the reader the truth of the statement. He clearly shows that Jesus is "*enthroned* not on the ark or cherubim, but *on the cross*."[21]

---

17. Chronis, "The Torn Veil," 110.
18. Martin, *Mark—Evangelist and Theologian*, 213.
19. Dowd and Malbon, "The Significance," Ibid.
20. Mark 15:26.
21. Chronis, "The Torn Veil," 114.

(author's italics) This is the ultimate sign. No doubt, the meaning and the purpose of the crucifixion would be validated by the resurrection, yet it was the cross that was the culmination and fulfillment of Jesus' commission.[22]

This brings us back to the foot of the cross where the centurion is standing. He does not know, nor would he care about the tearing of the curtain. He has seen how Jesus died, though. He has seen the darkness covering the land during the middle of the day. The centurion also knows that Jesus is not being tried as a common criminal. He is not being accused of murder or theft; He is accused of being "The King of the Jews." The centurion has heard the taunts of the religious leaders, as well as passersby and the other condemned criminals. Through it all, Jesus did not answer them a word.

After enduring the agony for six hours, Jesus uttered a loud cry and "breathed his last." Mark does not tell us what Jesus uttered but he clearly portrays it as a "victor's cry of triumph."[23] While most people who were crucified grew weaker and weaker until they quietly died, Jesus shows that He was in control until the very end.[24] With His last breath He gave a shout of triumph and then voluntarily gave up His spirit. His manner of death fulfilled His own words when He said He came "to give his life as a ransom for many."[25] Jesus's life was not taken from Him. He gave it voluntarily fulfilling Isaiah's prophecy that, "he poured out his life unto death, and was numbered with the transgressors. For he bore the sin of many..."[26] Only in the resurrection would the ultimate meaning of Jesus's death be seen. Jesus knew clearly, though, that there could be no resurrection without enduring the agony of the crucifixion.

As the centurion watched Jesus die, he said, "Surely, this man was the Son of God!" It is unclear exactly what he meant by his exclamation. Johnson believes that a better translation of this verse would be, "Truly, this man was God's son."[27] As to what he meant, Lane says that

---

22. Tannehill, "The Gospel of Mark," 88.
23. Cole, *Mark*, 323. See also Brooks, *Mark*, 262.
24. Brooks, ibid.
25. Mark 10:45.
26. Isaiah 53:12.
27. Johnson, "Mark 15.39," 410. See also, Schmidt, *The Gospel of Mark*, 147.

God's Greatest Sign

he "presumably meant that Jesus was a divine man or deified hero who accepted humiliation and death as an act of obedience to a higher mandate."[28] At the same time, however, Mark clearly intended his readers to see in this exclamation a genuine Christian confession.[29] In any event, the reader knows that the centurion's confession is valid. His confession is a statement of faith, whether conscious or unconscious.[30] As we have seen over and over again throughout Mark's Gospel, as people encounter Jesus, and reach out to Him in faith, their lives are touched and healed. We do not know what happens to the centurion. Perhaps, as some early traditions assume, he did become a Christian. Mark does have him speak for all of us, however, who see the cross as God's greatest sign and most significant miracle.[31] If we are willing to see it through the eyes of faith, our lives will be transformed, also.

28. Lane, *Mark*, 576.
29. Ibid.
30. Cole, *Mark*, 324.
31. Martin, *Mark—Evangelist and Theologian*, 174.

26

The Resurrection

When the Sabbath was over, Mary Magdalene, Mary the mother of James, and Salome bought spices so that they might go to anoint Jesus' body. Very early on the first day of the week, just after sunrise, they were on their way to the tomb and they asked each other, "Who will roll the stone away from the entrance of the tomb?" But when they looked up, they saw that the stone, which was very large, had been rolled away. As they entered the tomb, they saw a young man dressed in a white robe sitting on the right side, and they were alarmed. "Don't be alarmed," he said. "You are looking for Jesus the Nazarene, who was crucified. He has risen! He is not here. See the place where they laid him. But go, tell his disciples and Peter, 'He is going ahead of you into Galilee. There you will see him, just as he told you.'" Trembling and bewildered, the women went out and fled from the tomb. They said nothing to anyone, because they were afraid.

(MARK 16:1–8)

WHILE THERE can be no doubt that the cross occupies the central place in Mark's Gospel, it is just as clear that the resurrection is the supernatural event that gives the cross its truest meaning. The resurrection reversed or overturned the results of the crucifixion, bringing life where there had been death. More importantly, however, the resurrection served to demonstrate the fact that God had vindicated Jesus as the, "pioneer of salvation for anyone believing in him."[1] The religious authorities clearly thought that they were doing God's will by eliminat-

---

1. Hurtado, *Mark*, 279.

The Resurrection

ing Jesus. By raising Jesus from the dead, God declared once and for all that He was the fulfillment of God's eternal plans and purposes.[2]

Mark's actual account of the resurrection is very brief. In fact, there are no accounts of post-resurrection appearances of Christ to His disciples.[3] When placed alongside the other miracles and supernatural events in this Gospel, the resurrection event lacks detail and specifics. It is very tame in comparison to the other miraculous accounts. The brevity of the account has puzzled readers since the days of the early Church.[4] As it is, the ending of Mark's Gospel leaves the reader hanging. This may have been the result that Mark intended. Some have speculated as to whether or not Mark actually intended for the book to end here.[5] Perhaps he intended to come back and finish it later. At any rate, it does end at verse 8 and this is what we have to work with.

The main characters in this chapter include three women: Mary Magdalene, Mary, the mother of James and Joses, and Salome, and "a young man." These are the three same women whom Mark identified as "watching from a distance" at the crucifixion.[6] Two of them, Mary Magdalene and Mary the mother of James and Joses were also present at Jesus's internment.[7] As they approach the tomb, early on the morning after the Sabbath, they realize that they are not going to be able to gain access due to the large stone covering the entrance. When they arrive at the tomb, however, they observe that the large stone has been rolled away. It will become clear that the stone was not removed to let Jesus out. Other Gospel accounts, in His encounters with His

2. Kingsbury, *Conflict in Mark*, 55.
3. Cole, *Mark*, 331.
4. A study of the "long ending" of Mark is beyond the scope of this book. Suffice it to say that the "long ending" is not present in the earliest manuscripts and scholars almost universally understand Mark's Gospel to end at verse 8. This is not to cast aspersions on the validity of verses 9–20 as Scripture, however. The passage may well be a valid account of Jesus's post resurrection appearances and teaching. It just does not appear to belong at the end of Mark. Cole (335) draws a comparison with this passage and John 8:1-11. This is another example of a "misplaced story."
5. Hendriksen, *Mark*, 687.
6. Mark 15:40.
7. Mark 15:47.

followers, have the resurrected Jesus appearing and disappearing, often seeming to pass through doors and walls.[8] Here in Mark 16, the stone has been rolled away to permit entry into the now empty tomb. Without hesitation, the women enter the tomb.

Inside, they are confronted by the other character in this account, "a young man wearing a white robe." There is little doubt that Mark understood this figure to be an angel.[9] His white robe is one indicator, but the primary indicator is the fact that he communicates revelation to the frightened women. He knows their thoughts and intentions. He knows they are looking for Jesus but announces, "He has risen!" By way of emphasis, the angel then encourages the women to, "See the place where they laid him." There is no one there.

The presence of the angel gives weight to the fact that the tomb is empty. The empty tomb itself would not have been an indicator to the women that Jesus was alive. The women would just be wondering what had happened to His body.[10] They had seen Him die. People did not just walk away from being crucified. The women did not come to the tomb anticipating the resurrection. The angel's announcement that Jesus had risen provided the women with the revelation to go along with the empty tomb.

The angel's presence also served to underscore "the eschatological character of the resurrection of Jesus,"[11] as well as anticipating His return "when he comes in his Father's glory with the holy angels."[12] In Luke's Gospel, angels announced the birth of Jesus to a group of shepherds. In Mark's Gospel, angels ministered to Jesus during His wilderness testing, just after His baptism.[13] It is appropriate that an angel should be the one to announce the fact that Jesus had risen.

The angel entrusts the women with the message of Jesus's resurrection. They are instructed to go and "tell his disciples and Peter, 'He is going ahead of you into Galilee. There you will see him, just as he told you.'" The disciples had deserted Jesus and fled, leaving Him to

8. Luke 24:31, 36; John 20:19, 26.
9. Lane, *Mark*, 587; Brooks, *Mark*, 270.
10. See John 20:10–15.
11. Lane, ibid.
12. Mark 8:38. See also Mark 13:26–27.
13. Mark 1:12–13.

The Resurrection

His fate on the night of His arrest.[14] Peter had denied knowing Jesus three times. The angel's words here convey forgiveness and the restoration to fellowship.[15] The disciples will see Jesus again on this side of eternity. This is the message that the angel entrusts to the women.

The next verse, however, seems to imply that the women disobeyed the angel's directive. "They said nothing to anyone, because they were afraid." In reality, we know from the other Gospels that the women did tell the disciples what they had seen and heard. Hendriksen understands this verse to mean that the women did not stop on the way to talk with anyone because they were afraid.[16] Mark's narrative does end, though, on a note that would leave the reader wondering what happened, if they were not already familiar with the story. Did the women pass the message on to the disciples as the angel directed them? Did they eventually encounter the resurrected Jesus?

It is intriguing that Mark would end his Gospel on this note of human fear and weakness. At the same time, however, this has been a recurring theme throughout his Gospel. The resurrection is the culmination of a theme that Mark has developed at length in his book. That theme is the fact that divine power can overcome human weakness. Over and over again, Jesus demonstrated the power of God against sickness, demonic possession, and even nature itself. When confronted by the shocked and grief stricken father who had just lost his daughter, Jesus told Jairus, "Don't be afraid; just believe." To the father of the severely possessed boy, Jesus told him, "Everything is possible for him who believes." Here, the resurrection takes what appears to be the ultimate defeat and turns it into the ultimate victory.

---

14. Mark 14:50.
15. Brooks, *Mark*, 271.
16. Hendriksen, *Mark*, 681.

Bibliography

Achtemeier, Paul J. *Mark*. Proclamation Commentaries, ed. Gerhard Krodel. Philadelphia: Fortress Press, 1986.

———. *Invitation to Mark: A Commentary on the Gospel of Mark with Complete Text from the Jerusalem Bible*. New York: Image Books, 1966.

Bock, Darrell L. *Luke*. The NIV Application Commentary, ed. Terry Muck. Grand Rapids: Zondervan, 1996.

Brooks, James A. *Mark*. The New American Commentary, ed. David S. Dockery. Nashville: Broadman Press, 1991.

Carroll, John T. and Joel B. Green. *The Death of Jesus in Early Christianity*. Peabody: Hendrickson Publishers, 1995.

Chronis, Harry L. "The Torn Veil: Cultus and Christology in Mark 15:37-39." *Journal of Biblical Literature* 101/1 (1982) 97-114.

Cole, R. Alan. *Mark*. Tyndale New Testament Commentaries. Leon Morris, editor. Leicester: Inter-Varsity Press, 1989.

Dowd, Sharon and Elizabeth Struthers Malbon. "The Significance of Jesus' Death in Mark: Narrative Context and Authorial Audience." *Journal of Biblical Literature* 125, no.2 (2006) 271-97.

English, Donald. *The Message of Mark*. The Bible Speaks Today, ed. John R. W. Stott. Downers Grove: InterVarsity Press, 1992.

Eve, Eric. "Spit in Your Eye: The Blind Man of Bethsaida and the Blind Man of Alexandria." *New Testament Studies* 54 (2008) 1-17.

Feyerabend, Karl. *Langenscheidt Pocket Dictionary Classical Greek*. Berlin: Langenscheidt.

France, R. T. *Divine Government: God's Kingship in the Gospel of Mark*. Vancouver: Regent College Publishing, 1990.

Fuller, R. H. *Interpreting the Miracles*. London: SCM Press LTD, 1963.

Garrett, Susan R. *The Temptations of Jesus in Mark's Gospel*. Grand Rapids: Eerdmans Publishing, 1998.

Grudem, Wayne. *Systematic Theology—An Introduction to Biblical Doctrine*. Grand Rapids: Zondervan Publishing, 1994.

Gundry, Robert H. *A Survey of the New Testament*. Grand Rapids: Zondervan Publishing, 2003.

Harrisville, Roy A. *The Miracle of Mark*. Minneapolis: Augsburg Publishing House, 1967.

Bibliography

Hawkin, David J. "The Incomprehension of the Disciples in the Marcan Tradition." *Journal of Biblical Literature* 91 (1972) 491–500.
Hendrickson, William. *Mark*. New Testament Commentary. Grand Rapids: Baker Books, 1975.
Hurtado, Larry W. *Mark*. New International Biblical Commentary, ed. W. Ward Gasque. Peabody: Hendrickson Publishers, 1989.
John, Jeffrey. *The Meaning in the Miracles*. Grand Rapids/Cambridge: William B. Eerdmans Publishing Company, 2001.
Johnson, E. S. "Mark VIII. 22–26: The Blind Man from Bethsaida." *New Testament Studies* 25, 370–83.
———. "Mark 10:46–52: Blind Bartimaeus." *The Catholic Biblical Quarterly* 40 (1978), 191–204.
———. "Mark 15.39 and the So-Called Confession of the Roman Centurion." *Biblica* 81 (2000), 406–13.
Johnson, Luke Timothy. *The Writings of the New Testament—An Interpretation*. Minneapolis: Fortress Press, 1999.
Juel, Donald H. *Mark*. Augsburg Commentary on the New Testament. Minneapolis: Augsburg Publishing House, 1990.
Kelber, Werner H. *Mark's Story of Jesus*. Philadelphia: Fortress Press, 1979.
Kingsbury, Jack Dean. *Conflict in Mark—Jesus, Authorities, Disciples*. Minneapolis: Fortress Press, 1989.
Lane, William. *Commentary on the Gospel of Mark*. The New International Commentary on the New Testament. Grand Rapids: Eerdmans Publishing, 1974.
Lewis, C. S. *The Lion, the Witch and the Wardrobe*. New York: Harper Entertainment, 1950.
Martin, Ralph. *Mark—Evangelist and Theologian*. Grand Rapids: Zondervan Publishing, 1972.
Morris, Leon. *1 Corinthians*. Tyndale New Testament Commentaries. R. V. G. Tasker, editor. Leicester: Inter-Varsity Press, 1958.
Moulton, Harold K. *The Analytical Greek Lexicon Revised 1978 Edition*. Grand Rapids: Zondervan Publishing, 1977.
Oden, Thomas C., and Christopher A. Hall, editors. *Ancient Christian Commentary on Scripture, New Testament: Mark*. Downers Grove: InterVarsity Press, 1998.
Richardson, Alan. *The Miracle Stories of the Gospels*. London: SCM Press LTD, 1941.
Schmidt, Daryl D. *The Gospel of Mark*. The Scholars Bible, eds. Robert W. Funk and Julian V. Hills. Sonoma: Polebridge Press, 1990.
Spell, David. *Peter and Paul in Acts*. Eugene: Wipf and Stock Publishers, 2006.
Tannehill, Robert C. "The Gospel of Mark as Narrative Christology." *Semeia* 57–95.

www.ingramcontent.com/pod-product-compliance
Lightning Source LLC
Chambersburg PA
CBHW070921160426
43193CB00011B/1551